I've been fortunate to have fantastic friends surround me in life. To Joe Cox, Eric Purvis, and Kris Billiter. No matter who they root for, they've always been on my team. Thanks, brothers!

—Ryan Clark

It was Adolph Rupp who said it, and Cawood Ledford who borrowed the line, but to those who traveled the Glory Road with me, my eternal thanks. But a VIP pass to my wife, Julie, who centers my life, probably because she is always at the heart of it, and to my Sunday school teacher, Dennis Smith, who can somehow challenge me and uplift me at the same time.

—Joe Cox

Contents

THE

KENTUCKY WILDCATS FANS'
BUCKET LIST

RYAN CLARK
AND JOE COX

TRIUMPH
BOOKS

This book is available in quantity at special discounts for your group or organization. For further information, contact:

Triumph Books LLC
814 North Franklin Street
Chicago, Illinois 60610
(312) 337-0747
www.triumphbooks.com

Printed in U.S.A.
ISBN: 978-1-62937-115-3
Design by Andy Hansen
Page production by Patricia Frey

Foreword

On February 21, 2015, University of Kentucky basketball great Tony Delk watched along with a Rupp Arena crowd of more than 24,000 as his jersey was lifted to the rafters, retired for all to see. Delk scored 1,890 points in his career, good for fifth on the all-time UK list. As a senior, he was a first-team All-American and the SEC's Player of the Year. After leading the 1996 Wildcats to the national title, where he was named Most Outstanding Player of the Final Four, he was drafted in the first round by the NBA's Charlotte Hornets. Delk went on to play in the NBA for 10 years. He is now a commentator for ESPN's SEC Network.

I've never seen a fan base like the one I saw when I was at the University of Kentucky. They're one of a kind. And they make you feel so special, even after your playing career is done. You just can't describe what that feeling is like. They took me—a kid from Tennessee—and welcomed me into the Big Blue family. And I've been forever grateful.

There are a couple of memories that really stand out for me that fans probably don't know about. These are things that I never really knew about Kentucky and Kentucky basketball, but when I experienced them, I was so glad I did. They were on my bucket list at UK.

One was the Kentucky Derby. After my freshman season, when we had gone to the Final Four, Walter McCarty and some of my other teammates and I went to the Derby in Louisville. I didn't see a horse, but man, did we have a great experience. That was really the first time I felt like a celebrity as a UK player. I mean, we weren't in Lexington, we weren't with students or anything. We were in another town, and people just came up to us and were so appreciative.

Another event is Midnight Madness. I went to my first Midnight Madness on my recruiting visit, and seeing how the fans were so crazy, and how big their commitment was to UK basketball, was unlike anything I'd imagined. I couldn't believe so many people would come out to a free game at midnight. And years later, when I was a senior, Walter and I came out dressed as Batman and Robin. We had these cables that would lower us to the ground and it looked pretty dangerous. I remember Coach Pitino was not happy about us doing it—because it looked like we could get hurt and we were getting ready for a national championship run—but we did it and people loved it.

If I could tell fans now what to do on their bucket list, it would be two things:

1. Follow the players on social media—Twitter, Facebook, etc.—and show them support. Don't be weird and post awful things if they lose. We didn't have these things when I was a player, but now, as a fan, you have a way to really be able to get to know these players. And, let's face it, these talented guys aren't staying until they're seniors, so we really don't get to know them as well as we used to. Following them on these networks can help with that. But keep it cool. Tell them how much you appreciate them.

2. Go to the Final Four and watch your team, if you ever get the chance. I remember when I was a freshman in New Orleans, and when I was a senior in New Jersey, all the people who came out to watch us in the Final Four, and how happy they were. Seeing 20,000 or 30,000 Kentucky fans in the Superdome when I was a freshman was just amazing—and terrifying. I wasn't playing a lot so I was pretty nervous. But by the time we made it back to the Final Four in 1996 it was more businesslike. We were there to win a national title.

For four years, Kentucky fans made me feel like I was right at home. People stop me all the time and talk to me about hitting a big three and getting fouled when we played Syracuse in the national championship game. We were able to win that title, which was one of things I knew I had to do while I was at Kentucky.

Similarly, this book tells you, the fan, what you need to do while following your team.

And from me to you, I just want to say thank you to all the fans who made me feel so appreciated along the way!

Go Big Blue!

—Tony Delk
March 2015

Acknowledgments

It's rare in life that someone comes to you and says, "Hey, we want you to write this book…" and then pays you to do it. Seriously. This never really happens.

But Joe and I are lucky, in a sense. We've created a bit of a niche here, and sometimes, when people have ideas about UK basketball books, they come to us. And sometimes (okay, most of the time) if we think the idea is a good one, and we think we can do something with it, we'll give it a go.

In 2014, Triumph Books came to me with an idea: a bucket list about UK basketball. I brought the idea to Joe, and we discussed it. We'd done something similar with Triumph before, but we saw where this could be a little more personal, something more like a memoir than a straight how-to book.

And of course, being a writer, I always feel it's better to be working on a project than not. Inevitably, people ask you, "So what are you working on now?" It's good to have an answer. But this wasn't just any book—this idea sounded like a quality one. What would we say to those people who wondered what exactly they needed to do (and see, and eat…) as a UK fan? Could we even do this?

After thinking about it for a while, we came up with a good working list of chapters and graphics. We thought this could be a really fun book.

And it is. It's been a blast to work on, and there are several people to thank. First, as always, I have to thank my wife, Manda, and my daughter, Carrington, who allow me to do these fun things. They have to put up with me and this UK sickness of mine. Sometimes it's fun. Other times…it may not be, and I thank them so much for letting me do this again.

Once more, thanks to Joe for the guidance and motivation. I found a great writing partner—others should be so lucky.

I have to thank the journalists, athletes, fans, coaches, authors, and staff who either helped us through interviews, or helped us find people to interview. We could not do this without you.

Thanks to Tim Sofranko, the best darn photographer who lives in my neighborhood, for his donated photos (once again, you saved our bacon, Tim).

And thanks to UK legend (and new television star) Tony Delk, who loved the idea of this book and wrote the foreword for us. You were always one of my favorites, Tony. Now you just moved up the list!

And to Noah Amstadter, and all those wonderful folks at Triumph, thanks again for the opportunity.

Last, but not least, when I think about writing this book I will always remember the 2014–15 UK basketball season. Never before have we been on a ride like the one led by the Harrison twins, Willie Cauley-Stein, Trey Lyles, Devin Booker, Dakari Johnson, Karl-Anthony Towns, Tyler Ulis, and the rest of that year's squad. I firmly believe 38–0 will never be accomplished by a major-conference team ever again. And just because the season ended with a surprise loss to Wisconsin, it will not ruin the memories of that incredible journey.

So thank you to all who made those memories possible. We will not forget them.

Go Big Blue!

—Ryan Clark
April 2015

Ryan covered it pretty well, but like the white platoon, I'm going to check in and do a little damage myself.

Thanks to Triumph for having such a great idea, to Noah for bringing it our way, and to Michelle Bruton for helping us try to figure out exactly what this bucket list should look like.

Thanks again to my wife, who isn't just a great wife, but a great reader/editor/marketing consultant. She wears many hats, and somehow always keeps her head.

Big hugs and love to my kids, Natalie and Ryan. I hope they always know that I'm on their team.

Gratitude is always due to Ryan Clark, not only for getting me into this writing racket, but for being a great friend. Working with him is always a pleasure.

I second Ryan on thanking those who have gone before—photographers, columnists, players, coaches, and fellow fans. Big Blue kudos to Linda Sinclair, for telling me about the women's clinic, and to Shannon Ragland, for sharing his info about the Calipari Experience camp. Thanks to Jim Porter, for telling me more about his Ohio UK Convention—and double thanks to Jim and Linda for sharing photos. If a picture is worth a thousand words, then I suppose you guys deserve several thanks for sharing not just your words, but photos.

Last, but definitely not least, thanks to everybody who has read any of my books. It really does mean a ton.

—Joe Cox
April 2015

Introduction

Key to the Book

"Key" sounded a little better than "how to read this book," but that's what I'm imparting here. Ryan and I picked our brains and UK-cluttered houses apart, and came up with a list of ultimate things to do, places to go, etc. Entries that require further instructions begin with a little text box giving you the bare bones of the topic.

The text box tells you where and when to do these things. Pretty straightforward stuff there. It also tells you how to do whatever it is that we're telling you to do. Next is the cost factor—we ranked those as follows:

Free

$= $1–$9 per person

$$ = $10–$99 per person

$$$ = $100–$999 per person

$$$$ = $1,000–$9,999 per person

$$$$$ = $10,000+ per person

We also included a "difficulty rating." This is just our attempt to tell you how hard it is to accomplish your UK-related task. We went to the traffic system on this one. ● means go, easy-peasy. ● means there are some things to know/consider. ● means stop and make sure this is viable for you.

Next comes the "bucket rank." We ranked the items from one to five buckets (five being most important) on how essential the items are to your fandom. Don't misunderstand; even the one-bucket stuff is great, or it wouldn't be in here. But all UK experiences aren't created equal.

Last, we tried to include tips for little/reluctant Wildcats. We're both married guys with young kids. If you're going to drag your family along, we wanted to make it a little more fun for them.

We broke the book down geographically into six sections. Each section begins with a title page giving you an idea of what it involves, and what some of the highlights are. Complete the list and you receive...well, our envy. We haven't finished the list yet ourselves. But it's early!

The one absolute biggest rule of all is: have fun. That's what this book is about.

Chapter 1

The Ultimate Game Day Experience

It wouldn't be a Kentucky Wildcats bucket list without seeing a basketball game at Rupp Arena. But we're not just dumping you out and telling you "go see a game." No way. We're telling you where to go before, where to go after, what to watch for, what songs to sing, what to eat, who to talk to...believe us, when you're done, you will have had the ultimate game day experience!

Watch a Game in Rupp Arena

WHERE: Downtown Lexington, Kentucky.

WHEN: November until March

HOW TO DO IT: Connections/Money/the Internet/Scalpers/the UK box office at certain times

COST FACTOR: Solidly $$ or $$$ per person, maybe closer to $$$$ if you want a prime seat.

DIFFICULTY FACTOR: Sometimes not as difficult as you would think. ▌ for big games. ▌ for some mediocre conference games. ▌ for easy teams and preseason contests.

BUCKET RANK: 🗑 🗑 🗑 🗑 🗑

HINTS FOR LITTLE WILDCATS/RELUCTANT WILDCATS:
There are many things throughout the experience to do and see for little Wildcats fans. Bring your ball—as you will see why. Girls can dress in their little UK cheerleader uniforms. See the Lexington castle. Have some ice cream (a must for kids and adults) and burgers afterward. Some children may be put off by the noise, but in general, Rupp crowds are not known for their boisterousness. In general, the crowd is nice and kid friendly.

• •

A bucket list for University of Kentucky fans has to begin with a trip to Rupp Arena to see the Wildcats play basketball. Whether it's a top-ten matchup, a rivalry battle, or a conference game, seeing a contest in person in the home arena has to be first on anyone's list.

After all, every fan—young or old—remembers watching his or her first game from the stands.

Here's the story of my first game.

I was lucky. Like those stories you hear from old-timers who talk about being little kids and climbing the fence to see the Red Sox or sneaking inside to see the Knicks, I also have a story about seeing my favorite team when I was young.

Like I said, I was lucky.

In the early 90s, when I was about 12 and my UK fandom was firmly taking hold, my aunt worked as a professional in the marketing office of the University of Kentucky's student newspaper, the *Kentucky Kernel*. She'd help them with promotions. Back in the day, when people actually read newspapers, sometimes the student section at Rupp Arena would hold up their newspapers and pretend to read them as the opposing team's starting five was being introduced. It was a jab at them—like, "Hey, we're not paying any attention to you." And when the starting five had all been announced, the students would normally then wad up their papers and throw them in the direction of the court. It was all in good fun.

Well, someone had to pass out those newspapers—thousands of them, one for every student. My aunt recruited me and my relatives to help.

So, for my first-ever game in Rupp, we showed up hours before tip-off and we passed out those newspapers. All of them. And what did we get for our effort? Media passes for the game. We didn't necessarily have seats, but we were in the building. And if you were a little kid, you could easily get accepted into the student section, which at the time was in the nosebleed section of the arena.

So I was there. I was in. And the game was actually a pretty big deal, which is why it called for the newspaper promotion. In 1991–92, Kentucky and the other league schools welcomed South Carolina and Arkansas into the Southeastern Conference. At the time, South Carolina was not an amazing basketball school, but Arkansas, led by fiery coach Nolan Richardson, had been talented for years. He was really building a program.

On January 25, 1992, UK hosted Arkansas for the first time in the new conference lineup. Kentucky, fresh off probation, had reclaimed a spot in the AP top 10, while the Razorbacks were ready to show everyone in America that they were the new power in the SEC. It was No. 8 Kentucky vs. No. 9 Arkansas: the old vs. the new.

Of course, I wasn't necessarily aware of all that then. I knew it was a big game. I knew Arkansas was good. I knew I was lucky to be there.

Still, with more than an hour before game time, I had other things on my mind. Armed with a pen and a giant "3" sign (which we also distributed out on fans' seats) I used my media pass to roam the court as the teams participated in their pregame shootarounds. At times I was just feet away from some pretty legendary players: Richie Farmer. John Pelphrey. Jamal Mashburn.

So, as they all came off the court, I got them to sign my poster. I was thrilled. Some stopped, while others walked by, hurrying into the locker room for coach Rick Pitino's pregame speech. The minutes were dwindling and even I got the sense the players didn't want to be late for Pitino.

But I really wanted Mashburn's autograph. Badly. He was the future NBA star. As he walked by me, I looked up.

"Mr. Mashburn?" I called out, meekly.

He didn't notice me, and kept walking down a hallway to a locker room.

"Boy, you'd better hustle," an older man said to me. He was wearing a blue sport coat and as he looked at the media credential around my neck, I could tell he knew I wasn't really any member of the media. "Go on now," he gestured to me. "Be quick."

Adolph Rupp, a Kansas native, learned basketball strategy by playing under coaching legends Phog Allen and James Naismith, who invented the game. By the time he retired at UK, he had won more college basketball games than any other coach. (Ryan Clark)

I nodded, now filled with moxie after the blue-coated man's encouragement (more on the Blue Coats later). I ran up to Mash and made sure to get just in front of him before he entered the locker room—where media were not allowed to go. I asked him again if he would sign my poster, and—even though it may have made him a few seconds late—he stopped to sign.

As he did I peered in the locker room area to see Pitino scrawling some notes on a dry-erase board. All the other players were there. "Where's Mash?" he asked no one in particular. The coach then looked over and saw Mashburn handing back my pen and poster. I thanked him but got interrupted.

"Get your ass in here right now!" Pitino screamed at the star, and Mash obeyed without showing any emotion. With that, he went inside, and some assistants shut the door, just like the last scene from *The Godfather*.

I'm sure Mash got chewed for a moment, but I was feeling pretty good about myself. I took my poster up to the student section, and they took care of me during the game. It was a great environment.

However, it was not a great performance by the Wildcats. I still can't decide whether or not I'm to blame.

Mashburn would go on to score his season-low in points: four. Led by Todd Day, Lee Mayberry, and Oliver Miller, Arkansas came into Rupp that day and let the world know there was a new force to be reckoned with in the SEC. The Razorbacks won 105–88.

As I headed out to the car with my family that day I was a bit disappointed because of the loss. But I had my poster with its autographs, and it wouldn't be the last time I passed out papers for a free seat at Rupp Arena.

No one forgets his first UK game.

—Ryan

My first game experience might not have been as dramatic as Ryan's, but in its own way, it was just as memorable. The tickets were a Christmas present from my friend Carlton Hughes, who gets double credit for also taking me to my first UK football game. Carlton is a

A CLOSER LOOK AT ADOLPH RUPP

Who: The man who made Kentucky basketball successful, and won four NCAA Tournament titles in Lexington.

Why: Before going to a game, it makes the most sense to learn a little bit about the man for whom the arena is named.

Where to Find Rupp: He's deceased, but there's a section later in the book about paying respects at his grave.

Rupp Arena opened in 1976 as the largest sporting event facility in the country. It was named for the most successful coach in college basketball: Adolph Rupp, who led the Kentucky Wildcats from 1930 to 1972 and amassed a record of 876–190 with four national championships. Rupp was named national coach of the year five times and made six trips to the Final Four.

From Halstead, Kansas, Rupp played at the University of Kansas for the legendary Phog Allen (James Naismith, who invented the game of basketball, was an assistant coach for the team at the time). So Rupp came from basketball royalty, and he brought a little (or a lot) of that with him to Kentucky. His teams were known for their fast pace and tough defense, and in 1969, Rupp was enshrined in the Basketball Hall of Fame.

Rupp died of cancer in 1977 at the age of 76. On the night he passed away, Kentucky defeated Kansas in a college basketball game on "Adolph Rupp Night."

He is buried in Lexington Cemetery, just down the road from the arena that bears his name. More on that topic later.

community college professor in the KCTCS system, and he nabbed tickets for a random December game at Rupp.

Kentucky played Tulsa, and our seats were in the corner of the lower level of the arena. We did end up sitting in front of the two dozen Tulsa fans who ended up in Lexington. This led to some clever repartee during the game. I recall telling the Tulsa fans to "start the bus" in the middle of the second half.

This Kentucky team was led by new UK coach Tubby Smith, and was still struggling to find its identity. At halftime, Tulsa led by a point, mostly on the three-point shooting of a guard named Jonnie Gendron, who also pitched unsuccessfully in the Pittsburgh Pirates' farm system. In the second half, UK's talent and size took control, and the Wildcats eventually won 74–53 behind 17 points off the bench from Nazr Mohammed.

The interesting aspect of my first game lies in the history that no one could have ever predicted. Of course, Smith was a new coach at UK, and had formerly coached at Tulsa. Kentucky went on to win the NCAA title the following March. Tulsa also had a new coach, and he had not yet coached in an NCAA Tournament game, but you may have heard of him—his name was Bill Self. And Self, the future title-winning Kansas boss, was then assisted by… wait for it… future UK head coach Billy Gillispie, in his first trip to Rupp Arena. The game was a weird collision of basketball futures, and it ended up being decided by Nazr Mohammed and a lousy minor league baseball pitcher.

—Joe

Want to see Kentucky's collection of championship trophies? You can. You just have to walk into the Joe Craft Center and take a picture. (Ryan Clark)

Before the Game

Get there early. And this isn't just because of the Lexington traffic. But while we're talking about it, Rupp Arena is located in the very heart of downtown Lexington, and yes, on game day, there can be some wicked traffic, so you do want to avoid that, too. But that's not really the point. We want you to get there really early, like maybe a few hours before game time.

Why? Because there's a lot more entertaining stuff to do before you even get to the arena.

Get your gear on to make the trip. This means everything blue that you have to wear. Trust us—fans have seriously been made fun of for wearing something that shows fashion sense instead of fan sense. You never want to accidentally get caught in the colors of the opposing teams. So ditch the dress-up wear and come in comfortable shoes and all things blue.

Next, be sure to bring a basketball with you, preferably one of those nice ones with a white panel so people can sign an autograph on it. If you don't have one, there are several places you'll encounter to buy one, if you want. But it may come in handy.

Then—and especially if you have young kids—get in the car with your basketball and head outside the city. There, you can explore a bit of the Lexington countryside, whether it's the Kentucky Horse Park (during the holidays they offer beautiful displays of Christmas lights) or the legendary Castle Post in Versailles (also known as the Martin Castle or the Versailles Castle).

The Castle Post is now a bed-and-breakfast, but also serves as one of the most prominent sights in the area. Building began in 1969, and the castle has changed hands several times over the course of history. If nothing else, it makes for an amazing photo opportunity. When driving into downtown Lexington, my daughter loves to see it on the horizon.

"That's where Anna and Elsa live," my daughter said after seeing it for the first time. As we all know now, those are the princess sisters from the Disney movie *Frozen*.

—Ryan

While you're driving in, clad in blue, you need to make your way over to campus, where there are a few photo opportunities you don't want to pass up. Drive down the Avenue of Champions and you'll see a bronze Wildcat climbing on a tree branch. This is Wildcat Alumni

Plaza, and you'll be sure to want to take a picture with the cat. The bronze statue was originally an idea of the student community, and replicas can even be bought on the alumni website.

Across the street is legendary Memorial Coliseum, where the Wildcats played before moving to Rupp Arena. But we want to head around back.

Behind Memorial Coliseum you'll see a few sights no UK fan wants to miss. First, you'll notice a small strip of driveway between the coliseum and a student residence hall. This is Wildcat Coal Lodge, the posh space where UK students (including the entire men's basketball squad) live—just feet away from their practice facility.

The Wildcat Coal Lodge was renovated in 2012, with amenities for the college superstar.

The $7 million privately funded dorm (hence, the "Coal" in the name) features a private chef, as well as rooms designed specifically for 7'0" athletes (like having extra-long beds). You never know who you may see walking to and from the building. You're not allowed in, but maybe you'll sit for a spell next to a famous coach.

LEARN MORE ABOUT JOE B. HALL

Who: The only UK head coach in the modern era to have also played at UK; an NCAA champion (as a player and a coach); a Kentuckian; and a local folk hero.

Why: Because nobody gets Kentucky and Kentucky basketball quite as well as Coach Hall

Where to Find Hall: With his longtime radio gig finished, Coach Hall is mostly enjoying his retirement in and around Lexington. He's still around the program frequently, and is one of the more approachable legends in UK history.

Hailing from Cynthiana, Kentucky, Joe B. Hall was born and bred to coach the Wildcats. He played one season for a national champion Rupp team in 1948–49 ("I didn't really get to play that much," he's said, laughing), then left to finish his playing career at the University of the South. He then made coaching stops at Regis College, Central Missouri, and Kentucky before taking over for Rupp in 1972.

Hall went on to a 373–156 overall coaching record, took his UK teams to three Final Fours, and won the 1978 National Championship. That season he was named national coach of the year and in 2012 he was enshrined in the College Basketball Hall of Fame.

Many say you never want to be the guy who replaces a legend. But Joe B. Hall replaced Adolph Rupp and fared more than well. He would later go on to host a popular radio show with his longtime rival, former Louisville coach Denny Crum. The Joe B. and Denny Show aired from March 2004 to October 2014.

On September 18, 2012, UK unveiled a 400-pound bronze statue of legendary coach Joe B. Hall outside of the lodge. Sit on the same bench as the old coach and snap a selfie with the man who brought home the Wildcats' fifth national championship.

After sitting with Joe B. Hall, you should make your way back to the direction of the Coliseum. Around back you will notice a more modern-looking addition, with a sign that reads "Joe Craft Center."

Joe Craft, a native of Hazard, Kentucky, has a reported net worth of $1.4 billion from his diversified coal producing and marketing corporation. In 1976, Craft earned a law degree from UK. In 2007, Kentucky opened the 102,000-square foot, $30 million center, and Craft donated $6 million to the project.

The Joe Craft Center features state-of-the-art basketball practice facilities and offices. But it also houses the trophies for each of the eight national championships, as well as other memorabilia and photos. And here's the fun part: anyone can go in and look. Just walk in the front door during normal office hours and take some pictures.

It's time to head back toward Rupp Arena. But once you've parked, make sure and grab that basketball, if you've got one. As you're walking through the parking lots you may see a few folks tailgating, singing, and goofing off to pass the time. But the real fun is indoors.

No matter the entrance you go in, take time to walk around the first floor of the Lexington Center, which is connected to the arena. There you'll see shops, restaurants, and probably some free giveaways like spirit towels, posters, or buttons.

But you will definitely see hundreds of fans—chanting, laughing, and carrying on. These are the true fans, the ones who will come support the team no matter what. They will congregate in these areas to fraternize before the contest. And if you talk to anyone, be ready. More than likely, they'll be ready to educate you about Kentucky history. Then again, you'll be able to give tips of your own because you've read this book. Right? Let's move on.

MATT JONES/KENTUCKY SPORTS RADIO

Who: Jones is the most popular name in Kentucky sports media—a successful sports blogger, radio host, and sometimes sideline analyst for the UK Radio Network.

What: Kentucky Sports Radio refers to both Jones' blog and radio show. His media empire began with just a few friends writing on a blog, and over the past decade, the KSR brand has become a phenomenon.

Why: They're fans and they're fun. Jones and the KSR crew know their stuff and have a good time with their audience.

Where to Find Matt/KSR: See the KSR Tour Stop entry later in this book and visit KentuckySportsRadio.com.

There are few UK fans now that haven't heard of Matt Jones.

They listen to him on his radio show. They read his website. They see him on television talking about UK sports.

If you're lucky, you may even see some former players. In 2015, former stars Tony Delk, Mike Pratt, and Jack "Goose" Givens made appearances in that area to sign and sell artistic prints of their likenesses. Keep that ball (and maybe a Sharpie) handy.

Go over and grab some snacks from the food court. There, you'll be able to settle in and listen to the UK pregame radio show with local sports media legends Matt Jones, Drew Franklin, and Ryan Lemond. Known for their fun and knowledge, you will enjoy yourself and learn a bit about UK and their opponent.

Born in 1978, Matt Jones grew up in Cynthiana and Middlesboro, Kentucky. He graduated from Duke Law School and it looked as though he would practice law like his mother, who happens to be the Commonwealth Attorney in Bell County.

But something happened along the way, and Jones—who grew up rooting for the Cats with his grandfather—decided to start a sports-themed blog. In 2005, KentuckySportsRadio.com debuted, which led to radio and television hosting gigs. Now—after seemingly mastering the new-media world of blogging, tweeting, and posting videos—the website is the "largest independent sports blog in America," Jones says.

According to a 2013 interview with the *Lexington Herald-Leader*, the blog averages more than 150,000 unique visitors a day, with page views ranging from 180,000 to 220,000 on the most popular days.

His radio show is now broadcast on nearly 30 stations across the state. And he also hosts pre- and postgame radio shows for UK sports, as well as sideline reports from basketball games.

"My goal every day on the radio show and on the website is to give the consumer what they want," he told the paper.

There are shops within the Lexington Center where you can buy a basketball (or other memorabilia or apparel) if you haven't yet gotten one. But after listening to the pregame show and fraternizing with fans it's time to grab your ticket—you're ready to head into the arena.

But you still want to save some time. Because there are some people you need to meet.

When you walk in and show the workers your ticket, you'll also pass by booths selling more apparel or game programs. But what you really want to grab is some Rupp Arena soft-serve ice cream. Why?

Just because people say it's the best soft serve ice cream in the world, that's why.

"We're always busy," says a nice, white-haired woman who looks eerily similar to Betty White from *The Golden Girls*. "People just love this ice cream. They tell us all the time that they've heard how they need to try it, and then they keep coming back for more."

It's cold. It's rich. It's perfect.

As you're eating your delectable treat, you'll want to wander, either before or after the game, just to see who you can run into. Here are a few people to watch out for:

Superfan Bob Wiggins: For 68 years, the 86-year-old Falmouth, Kentucky, resident has been attending UK basketball games—more than 1,650 in all. And for one unbelievable streak, Wiggins went 19 years without missing a home or away game. He's become known throughout Big Blue Nation for quite a while. When Rick Pitino was coach he let Wiggins fly from game to game with the team. When the Cats won their eighth national title in 2012, senior Darius Miller gave Wiggins a piece of the championship net. Try to find him if you can—normally he's in a suit, not far behind the UK bench.

Boogie Man: They call him the Boogie Man, but his real name is Darren Moscoe. During the first or second television timeout of the second half at home games, he comes alive in Section 19. Moscoe will gyrate, lunge, and twist during the blaring of Tommy James' "Mony Mony" as fans laugh and cheer. He's earned quite a following, too. "Even some pretty girls have asked me (for a picture)," Moscoe, 48, told the *Lexington Herald-Leader*. Moscoe grew up battling seizures and even had a brain tumor removed. All the while he never fit in at school. Now he fits in fine. You can find him normally dressed in everything blue—including beads.

The Mascots: That's right—there are two of them, and you will see them running around during the whole game. You'll like meeting both of them. The first is the Wildcat, which was introduced during the 1976–77 season. More recently, the UK athletic department introduced Scratch, a more child-friendly mascot. You can tell he's cool and young because of his tennis shoes and ballcap. Both appear at all basketball and football games.

The Stars: No, not the folks on the court. UK basketball has always had a "place to see and be seen" element to it. Even if you go to watch basketball, if you pay close attention, especially to folks in the prime seats behind the bench and in the first few rows at Rupp Arena, there's no telling who you may see. Just a few folks who have been sighted over the years: William Shatner, Muhammad Ali, Ashley Judd, Eddie Montgomery, Josh Hutcherson, Steve Zahn, LeBron James, Jay-Z, Drake, Spike Lee, Magic Johnson, Farah Fath, Billy Ray Cyrus, Garth Brooks, and Paul O'Neill.

> ## EXTRA POINTS
>
> ### The Football Superfan
>
> There's Jim Brown, the amazing running back for the Cleveland Browns of the NFL. Then there's Jim Brown—a different Brown from Kentucky who became famous for attending 412 consecutive UK football games from 1945 to 2009.
>
> He's the UK football Superfan. In 2009, Brown was forced to pull out of trip to a game because at 90, he was stricken with what he thought may be the flu.
>
> But for years he was always there: section 129, row 41, seat 22. In 2010 he was included in an ESPN story about super fans from across the country.
>
> "I figure 'The Streak' is safe," he told the *Lexington Herald-Leader* in 2009.

The Men in Blue: Also known as the Blue Jackets or the Committee of 101. You don't have to look far to find a member of the Committee of 101. Clad in their blue blazers, black slacks, and warm smiles, they help usher at UK sporting events. In 1966, a group of 101 local IBM employees chipped in to send then-coach Adolph Rupp a good-luck telegram, and they even showed up to meet the team at the airport. That gave Rupp an idea. Their group would help at the Kentucky sporting events. Currently, the organization includes more than

300 Blue Jackets. They will help you to your seat, but even more important, they will tell you about that year's team—in comparison with others. These men have so much historical knowledge they can tell you who is the best and who is not. Ask them for their thoughts, then stand back and enjoy the stories.

If you've been able to go up to these gentlemen and engage them in conversation, then bravo. We salute you. You've undoubtedly gained some knowledge. We would also like you to explore your surroundings a bit before you take your seat. Besides the people in it, the arena itself offers a lot of character to go around.

Big Bertha: First, look up. There's a huge, beige-ish white sound system hanging from the ceiling. That's Big Bertha, legendary for being an eyesore at the arena since the massive building was erected in 1976. This cluster of speakers pumps out music to the crowd. Nothing is more iconic and symbolic in the arena than Bertha, which is rumored to be replaced in the future by a large video screen.

The retired jerseys: Next, look up farther. You're going to see a lot of jerseys. These are the university's proud collection of retired jerseys, a.k.a. the greatest players in UK history. Only the best are memorialized forever. Tony Delk, an All-American guard and National Champion in 1996, was the latest to have his jersey retired, in 2015.

UK Retired Jerseys:

Player	Seasons
Basil Hayden	1919–22
Burgess Carey	1924–26
Carey Spicer	1928–31
Adolph Rupp	Head Coach, 1930–72
Forest "Aggie" Sale	1930–33
00: John DeMoisey	1931–34
4: Layton Rouse	1937–40

26: Kenny Rollins	1942–48
15: Alex Groza	1944–49
12: Ralph Beard	1945–49
27: Wallace Jones	1945–49
22: Cliff Barker	1946–49
77: Bill Spivey	1949–51
30: Frank Ramsey	1950–54
6: Cliff Hagan	1950–54
16: Lou Tsioropolous	1950–54
42: Billy Evans	1951–55
20: Gayle Rose	1951–55
Cawood Ledford	Broadcaster, 1953–92
22: Jerry Bird	1953–56
44: Phil Grawemeyer	1953–56
50: Bob Burrow	1954–56
52: Vernon Hatton	1955–58
24: Johnny Cox	1956–59
Bill Keightley	Equipment Manager, 1962–2008
44: Cotton Nash	1961–64
10: Louie Dampier	1964–67
42: Pat Riley	1964–67
44: Dan Issel	1967–70
Joe B. Hall	Coach, 1972–85
35: Kevin Grevey	1972–75
21: Jack Givens	1974–78
53: Rick Robey	1974–78
4: Kyle Macy	1977–80
34: Kenny Walker	1982–86
32: Richie Farmer	1988–92
12: Deron Feldhaus	1988–92
34: John Pelphrey	1988–92
11: Sean Woods	1989–92
24: Jamal Mashburn	1990–93
00: Tony Delk	1992–96
Rick Pitino	Coach, 1989–97

You'll notice there are only two jerseys in the rafters not belonging to athletes or coaches. One of those is "Mr. Bill" or "Mr. Wildcat," **Bill Keightley**, Kentucky's equipment manager for 46 years. Keightley became, in his later years, almost as popular as the players. He was much more than an equipment manager, as he served as father figure, confidant, and comic relief for the athletes. Countless times, after a coach would ride a player to the point of frustration, Keightley was there with a smile—and probably a Coke or a candy bar from his closet-sized office. He was famous for his hatred of rival Louisville, and for his love of the UK players and staff. A member of three national championship teams (1978, 1996, and 1998), Keightley wore two of his three national championship rings—one on each hand—while keeping the third in his pocket.

It was my understanding that he would wear 1978 on one hand and 1998 on the other. He even showed them to me once and I took a picture of his hands with championship rings on each one. I asked him why the 1996 ring always had to be kept in his pocket, and he implied to me that it was because the '96 title was won by former coach Rick Pitino, who later would go on to coach the rival Louisville Cardinals. Mr. Bill did not like the Cardinals—not at all. So it made sense that the '96 ring would be the one to stay in the pocket.

Keightley was inducted into the Kentucky Athletic Hall of Fame, was featured on a Maker's Mark bourbon bottle, and had a university athletic award named in his honor. An avid Cincinnati Reds baseball fan, Keightley died in 2008 while getting off a bus to watch his Reds play on Opening Day. He fell, and a previously undiagnosed tumor on his spine caused internal bleeding. He has been memorialized in many ways, from K's outlined in black on UK jerseys to an early-season tournament that bears his name. "He was always there for you," UK star Kevin Grevey said. "There was no one like him—and he's going to be missed forever."

The other nonathlete in the rafters is longtime radio announcer **Cawood Ledford**, who for 39 years called play-by-play for Kentucky basketball and football games. He also called the NCAA Final Four for CBS and the Kentucky Derby for many years. The iconic voice from Harlan, Kentucky, was so well received for his vocal prowess that many fans would turn down the volume on their television sets and listen to Ledford on the radio. He was known for painting a picture of what was going on in the game, and he will forever be remembered his various ways.

In his last season, 1992, Ledford called what many remember as the greatest collegiate basketball game ever: No. 1 seed Duke versus No. 2 seed Kentucky in the regional finals of the NCAA

It's the one thing that will always put a smile on a fan's face—even during a loss. You have to try Rupp Arena's soft-serve ice cream. (Ryan Clark)

Tournament. And when Christian Laettner hit his memorable shot to win it, Duke coach Mike Krzyzewski walked over and congratulated Ledford on-air for his brilliant career. Earlier in the season, Indiana coach Bob Knight presented Ledford with a red IU sweater as a retirement gift. In 2001, UK named its basketball court in Ledford's honor. Across from the scorer's table, in blue, it reads "Cawood's Court." He won three Eclipse Awards for outstanding coverage of thoroughbred racing, was named the state's Sportscaster of the Year a record 22 times, and was inducted into the Kentucky Athletic Hall of Fame in 1987.

You'll also notice the jerseys representing championship coaches, including Rupp, Joe B. Hall, and Rick Pitino. Take note of the Pitino jersey, which—at least once in history—was almost taken down.

EXTRA POINTS

Cats in the Hall of Fame

Ten Wildcats have been enshrined in the Basketball Hall of Fame in Springfield, Massachusetts:

Adolph Rupp
Cliff Hagan
Frank Ramsey
Dan Issel
C.M. Newton (contributor)
Pat Riley
Adrian Smith (member of the U.S. Olympic team)
Rick Pitino
Louie Dampier
John Calipari

But first, some history: Pitino saved UK basketball, at a time when the program was at its lowest. In the late 1980s, UK basketball was under the microscope for various allegations of impropriety, including admitting athletes who had questionable test scores, paying players, and other recruiting violations. Around that time, an Emery Worldwide freight envelope popped open in California, revealing $1,000 in cash. The package was sent to the father of a UK recruit—supposedly by a Kentucky assistant—which is a big-time no-no.

The ensuing NCAA investigation resulted in probation for Kentucky—a loss of scholarships, a postseason ban for two years, and the team couldn't even appear on television for one season. Players left. Coaches and administrators were fired. The program was in shambles. *Sports Illustrated* published an issue with "Kentucky's Shame" on the cover.

Enter Pitino. Lured away from coaching the NBA's New York Knicks, Pitino (who had made his bones in college coaching Providence to the 1987 Final Four with point guard Billy Donovan) came to Lexington for the rebuilding job of a lifetime. He succeeded beyond anyone's wildest imaginations. Pitino took a ragtag group of Kentucky kids who weren't good enough to play anywhere else and made them into a top-10 team in two seasons—and he played a style the fans loved, pressing and shooting three-pointers.

Fans loved Pitino. He was almost a god in Kentucky.

By 1996 he had the best team in college basketball. They went the distance, winning UK's sixth national championship. Pitino was on top of the world, but there were always rumors he may return to the NBA to rebuild a franchise—the Lakers, maybe, or the Celtics. In 1997, UK almost repeated as champions, losing to Arizona in overtime. And later that spring, Pitino confirmed the rumors, leaving UK to become coach of the Boston Celtics.

Fans were, on average, okay with the move. They loved Pitino for what he'd accomplished. They hung his jersey in the rafters. And they were fine with the coach who was hired to replace Pitino: Tubby Smith. Smith even won a championship in his first season. Everything was fine—that is, until Pitino failed in Boston.

In 2001 he was fired from his head coaching position in Boston. Again, it was rumored that Pitino would return to college coaching. Three jobs became available: UNLV, Michigan, and (UK archrival) Louisville. Surely, UK fans thought, Pitino would not coach at his former team's rival.

He did. And immediately, everything changed. Pitino, the once-loved former coach and savior, became Public Enemy No. 1.

Larry Ivy, then–athletic director at UK, even suggested Pitino's jersey be taken down from the rafters. Cooler heads prevailed, and the jersey was left hanging.

But that never changed the way the fans felt about their former coach. It just made the Kentucky–Louisville rivalry better than it had ever been.

(And, for the record, through 2015 Pitino was just 5–11 against UK as coach of Louisville).

So think about that when you see Pitino's name hanging up there.

Ah, see the rest of the banners, with all those years on them? At Rupp, we only raise banners for Final Four appearances and national titles. You'll see 17 Final Fours and eight national champion declarations:

1942: Final Four	1993: Final Four
1948: National Champions	1996: National Champions
1949: National Champions	1997: Runners-up
1951: National Champions	1998: National Champions
1958: National Champions	2011: Final Four
1966: Runners-up	2012: National Champions
1975: Runners-up	2014: Runners-up
1978: National Champions	2015: Final Four
1984: Final Four	

· ·

The eRUPPtion Zone

Shift your gaze from the massive ceiling back to the floor. Under one of the baskets, you should see a group of students start forming together into a large, blue, massive, moving amoeba of a crowd.

This is the eRUPPtion Zone.

Students will watch the game from this vantage point while standing—and shouting—the entire time. Back in the day, student seating used to be located at the very tip-top of the arena (which may be where you're seated today). Critics claimed this was entirely too far away for the students to create any kind of "home court advantage" for UK. So, in November 2002, UK created a new space for students to make themselves heard.

John Astle, a North Carolina native, was actually the first student ever in the eRUPPtion Zone.

WHEN ESPN IS IN THE HOUSE

For some games, you may be lucky enough to see the ESPN *College GameDay* crew make the contest its featured Game of the Day. It's going to be 9:00 PM on a Saturday night. It's going to be a good matchup—probably Florida.

What it also means is a whole day of fun—even if you don't have tickets—because the *GameDay* crew will be televising live from Rupp Arena all day. You don't need a ticket to get in and be part of the crowd. Make a poster. Make yourself known. You'll have a blast.

You may even get to meet ESPN luminaries such as Jay Bilas, Seth Greenberg, and Jay Williams. Once, No. 1 UK fan Ashley Judd was also in the house. You knew it was a big deal at that point.

"It was going to be my first UK game as a student, so I got there a couple hours early," Astle told UKNOW. "I ended up being first in line!"

His father, also a UK alum, has a memorable UK athletics experience, too.

"My dad watched Adolph Rupp's last game as the UK coach, and he always has told me about that," Astle said. "So maybe one day I can tell my kids, 'Hey, I was the first student in the eRUPPtion Zone.'"

Nowadays you'll see the eRUPPtion Zone featured prominently on television broadcasts. Normally during the early stages in the game (watch for it!) a huge Kentucky flag is rolled out over the top of the entire section and waved crazily during a timeout. In the past it has said "Kentucky Basketball Never Stops." Sometimes it just says "Kentucky." It's great for pictures and you will not want to miss it.

GETTING TICKETS

1. Follow @UKTix on Twitter and Instagram for updates. You never know what kinds of contests, specials, or announcements you may need to know.

2. Get there early. What we mean here is get there early in the season. Preseason games (Transylvania and teams of the like) are a great way to see your favorite UK teams. These tickets are normally not very difficult to come by. Contact the ticket office (http://www.ukathletics.com/tickets/ or (800) 928-2287).

3. Look for other not-very-good teams. Further down the early-season schedule, there are always teams that may draw less than the normal huge crowd at Rupp Arena (Grand Canyon, or Sun Belt or Atlantic Sun teams, for instance). Watch for these games and make sure to keep following and calling the UK ticket office leading up to them to see if there may be unclaimed tickets.

4. December is a great time to go to a game. Frequently, UK schedules a game that is during the afternoon in the middle of the week. Because of the difficulty of traveling for most fans (who are at work), attendance is always spotty. Check out the schedule and look for a game like this.

5. The weather. You'll have to be on your toes for this one, but during the winter there are always a couple of games that occur during some kind of snow mess. Watch for these, and if you're able, you will find affordable tickets online because sometimes people just can't make it to the arena.

6. Tickets in the eRUPPtion Zone during winter break. Make note of when students will be leaving for their winter break. There are several times when the ticket office may announce eRUPPtion

Zone tickets, which are normally sold for about five bucks. The catch is you may have to get there in the morning to pick them up. Again—call and ask. You may get a great spot to watch the game.

7. StubHub, Guy on the Corner Tickets, etc. Check these reputable online ticket retailers for tickets. They will have them—and you can buy them—for a price.

To the right of the eRUPPtion Zone is another proud group that helps make the atmosphere at Rupp Arena second to none. It's the band, part of the UK School of Music. The Basketball Pep Band is made up of Woodwind and Brass students who have completed Marching Band in the fall semester. A 29-member road band travels to every SEC and NCAA Tournament.

One of the questions we're always asked is how to get tickets. UK tickets have been especially difficult to get as of late. But there are still ways to get it in at face value.

The Game

As the game nears its start, you'll take your seats and get comfortable. Finish that ice cream and take a look at the free program you probably picked up on the way in. You can take a look at the roster and see if your favorite player may grace the cover. There are a couple of statistics you may want to know heading in to the action.

Kentucky doesn't lose very often in Rupp Arena. Through the 2015 season, UK is 529–64 in 39 seasons. That means statistically, you're probably going home happy with a win. Coach John Calipari is even less likely to lose at home. His record is 102–4 in his six seasons. It is the best start to a coaching career for home wins in UK history (both Rupp and Pitino started off 94–6 in their first 100 home games). Bottom line: UK should win. Enjoy.

UK is smack dab in the thick of a crazy streak of three-pointers made in consecutive games. As of the beginning of the 2015–16 season, the Wildcats had gone 939 consecutive games (not including exhibitions) with at least one three-point field goal made. This is second in the country to UNLV. But since we don't care about UNLV, let's focus on the Cats. That's more than 900 games! That goes back to 1986. Some of you readers probably weren't born yet—yes, that means UK has hit a three in every basketball game in your entire lifetime. The streak was challenged, however, most recently in a December 2014 game against Eastern Kentucky. Even though the Wildcats were up by 26, they had yet to hit a three—until (of course) Aaron Harrison canned one with under three minutes to play. So watch for it in the game. When will Kentucky hit a three to continue the streak?

Next, you'll hear the national anthem, which is normally sung by a member of the talented UK School of Music, or maybe another local music luminary (or fan). And here's where the fun begins. If you've never seen it before, again—you may want to get the cameras ready.

The UK athletic marketing department does a fantastic job with introduction videos for the home basketball games. Incorporating clips of the program's most exciting plays (contemporary examples include Boogie Cousins' game-tying putback in the 2010 SEC Tourney championship, Jodie Meeks scoring 54 points against Tennessee, and any shot by Aaron Harrison in an NCAA Tournament game) with hip-hop music sure to get your booty shaking, it all leads up to the lights going out, and the starters being introduced.

Don't be scared—sometimes flames shoot out of the basketball goals, illuminating the dark. I'm sure opposing teams have to be intimidated by all this. It's an impressive thing to see.

Near the last media timeout at the end of a game, the UK cheerleaders form a pyramid with a giant 'K' flag. Get your cameras ready—it only comes around once, but it's a great photo opportunity. (Ryan Clark)

Then, of course, the game begins. Have fun—and our advice to you: stand up and cheer. The hometown crowd in Rupp is constantly criticized for not standing up and cheering enough. Please do this. The team loves it.

At halftime, there are a couple other cool things to take note of. As the other fans trudge off to the bathrooms, you can check out the most successful athletic team on the UK campus. (By the way, who waits to do this now? Everyone knows going to the bathroom at halftime of a sporting event is the WORST idea. That's when everyone does it.)

Of course, I'm talking about the cheerleading squad, which just happens to be one of the most successful athletic teams anywhere in the country. If you don't know about them, you need to. And you need to pay attention to and cheer for them.

In 2014, the cheerleading squad won their 20th national championship. Yes, 20—more than any other Division 1A school. "UK's squad is the only team to win back-to-back championships three times, once in 1987 and 1988, again in 1995 and 1996, and a third time in 2008, 2009, and 2010," UK's official website says. "Further, UK is the only squad ever to win three, four, five, six, seven, and eight championships in a row. UK's eight-year streak of championships was broken in 2003 when they finished runner-up to Central Florida. They regained the title in January 2004 and won their third straight in 2006. Central Florida regained the championship in 2007 when UK finished in third place. But the next year, UK came home with their 16th title." Of course, they've added four more championships since, just for good measure.

Also worth watching is the UK Dance Team, which is composed of two teams: the Blue, which performs at men's basketball and football games, and the White, which performs at women's basketball and football games.

In the past few years, the team has finished in the top 10 in various Universal Dance Association events, including 5th in the nation in Hip Hop in 2014, and 6th in the nation in Hip Hop and 8th in the nation in Pom in 2013.

Check 'em out.

As you're watching the cheerleaders and dance team you'll probably want to know the words to the UK Fight Song. Written in the 1920s by Carl A. Lambert, first chairman of the Music Department, the song will be sung approximately a million times during the game. Because we're nice, we'll just go ahead and put the words here for you (courtesy of the UK Campus Guide):

On! On! U of K
On, on, U of K, we are right for the fight today,
Hold that ball and hit that line;
Ev'ry Wildcat star will shine;
We'll fight, fight, fight, for the blue and white
As we roll to that goal, Varsity,
And we'll kick, pass and run, 'till the battle is won,
And we'll bring home the victory.

During a timeout near the end of the (predictable) UK win, there will be another great photo opportunity to watch for. It's the UK flag and pyramid, built by the cheerleaders, the mascot, and another giant flag, this one showing a huge blue-and-white K. The band will also play as the pyramid is built—and be ready with your camera, as the entire setup will rotate 360 degrees, allowing all in the arena to see it from the front. Popular music played during the spectacle includes the theme from *2001: A Space Odyssey.*

· ·

After the Game

For the end of Kentucky's victory, you may want to learn some of the words to Kentucky's state song, "My Old Kentucky Home."

As the players go and shake their opponents' hands following the game, all of the cheerleaders link arms and sing a portion of the tune to the crowd, swaying while holding up one index finger to let everyone know who rules college basketball.

Need some help on the words? Once again, we're here for you. Memorize this:

My Old Kentucky Home, Good-Night!
The sun shines bright in My Old Kentucky Home,
'Tis summer, the people are gay;
The corn-top's ripe and the meadow's in the bloom
While the birds make music all the day.

The young folks roll on the little cabin floor,
All merry, all happy and bright;
By 'n' by hard times comes a knocking at the door,
Then My Old Kentucky Home, good night!

Chorus

Weep no more my lady
Oh weep no more today;
We will sing one song
For My Old Kentucky Home
For My Old Kentucky Home, far away

The song was adopted by the state legislature as the Kentucky state song in 1928 and the lyrics were updated in 1986. It was written by Stephen Foster in 1853, reportedly inspired by Federal Hill, the home of his Rowan cousins in Bardstown, Kentucky.

One of the great traditions in UK basketball was former Kentucky Governor A.B. "Happy" Chandler (1898–1991) singing "My Old Kentucky Home" on UK's Senior Day to the departing players. It was described by announcer Tom Hammond as "one of the most emotional moments in sport." UK star Kenny Walker was seen crying during the song. "Not a dry eye in the house" was how former U.S. Representative Ben Chandler, grandson of Happy, described Senior Day 1988 to the *Lexington Herald-Leader*. "(Happy) loved it. He loved it almost like nothing else."

Google the performance. You won't be disappointed.

Back in the old days, when college basketball teams actually had seniors, there was something called Senior Day, and it celebrated those special players who stayed and played all four years at their universities. At UK, of course it was more special than others.

In 2015, UK actually had three seniors: Brian Long, Sam Malone, and Tod Lanter, each of whom participated in the Wildcats' Senior Day festivities. If you're lucky enough to attend a Senior Day, you'll see a bevy of other activities before the game, including each senior running through a huge hoop with his face on it.

The player will then walk out to midcourt with his family and receive a loud ovation from the crowd. Typically, players receive a framed

Check out the most successful athletic team on UK's campus—the cheerleading squad, which won its 20th national championship in 2014. (Tim Sofranko)

jersey and portrait of them playing—and they will try not to cry. At the end, the seniors will link arms with the cheerleaders and sing "My Old Kentucky Home" as they walk off the court for the last time.

I was fortunate enough to attend two special Senior Day moments: for the Unforgettables squad (which I attended with my granddad) of John Pelphrey, Deron Feldhaus, Sean Woods and Richie Farmer in 1992; and for Chuck Hayes and Josh Carrier in 2005.

To be able to attend the Unforgettables' Senior Day was so special—I even knew it then when I was just a little kid. I knew how big of a deal it was. I have great memories from that day—it was the only game I've ever been to with my granddad, and we got these Rally Rags, with all the players' names on them. I still have mine hanging up on a wall in my house. Of course, one of the other great memories was this was Cawood Ledford's last game at home as a radio announcer.

But something else made the game stand out.

During Sean Woods'—now the coach at Morehead State—Senior Day at UK they were playing Tennessee, and Sean got thrown out for fighting. I couldn't believe it. He'd just gone through all this emotional stuff in the pregame, and UK comes out and starts handing it to the Vols and Sean gets thrown out of his Senior Day.

In 2005, the game was memorable for a different reason.

My wife is not a basketball fan, but I'd convinced her to come to Senior Day to pay our respects to the great career of Chuck Hayes. So we go to the arena and watch the game and—of course—we win, and through it all, we're having a great time. Everything is fine. At the end of the game, Chuck Hayes comes over and they start to sing "My Old Kentucky Home" with the cheerleaders. We see that big old Chuck is crying as he waves goodbye to the crowd.

And I look over and my wife is crying too. She hates when

EXTRA POINTS

John Short

If you're listening to the radio call-in shows, you may come across some characters—these are regular callers, people who have been calling in to talk to the different radio hosts over the past 20 years. They make a habit of letting their opinions be known—even if they say the same thing with virtually every call.

One of these characters is John Short. Short, who lives in Lexington and works bagging groceries at the Romany Road Kroger, has been legally blind since age 5, which means he makes a habit of listening to all the radio shows—and calling in to them.

Despite his handicap, he's done a lot in life. He's thrown out the first pitch for the Lexington Legends baseball squad. He covered a UK women's basketball game in 2012. He's been interviewed by the *New York Times*. He is, in a way, Kentucky basketball fan royalty.

"His love for UK sports began with Jack Givens," Tina Cox wrote for the VaughtsViews.com website. "It makes sense that his favorite players are Kyle Macy and Jack Givens and Joe B. Hall is his all-time favorite coach. He follows all UK sports but basketball is his favorite. He had nothing bad to say about any coach or player. He explained they all have 'good' in them."

Listen for him—he'll make any fan smile.

I tell this story, and she tries to deny that she cares—but she was moved by the moment.

This is the point, after the game, when you're going to want to take your ball (remember your basketball?) and move down toward the court. Just walk down—the Men in Blue are cool with it. Everyone moves down.

Just go walk on the court. Take a selfie with all the banners in the background. You'll love it.

TOM LEACH
AND MIKE PRATT

Who: Leach and Pratt are the current UK Radio Network broadcasters for all UK games. Leach is a longtime broadcaster, and Pratt is a former UK All-American who serves as color commentator.

Why: These guys are one of the best teams in UK history. They bring the action home to thousands, if not millions, across the state, nation, and globe.

Where to Find Leach and Pratt: They are, generally, wherever the team is—particularly notable in the Rupp postgame festivities.

Tom Leach is the latest in a long line of legendary broadcasters to call UK basketball and football games. First, there was Claude Sullivan, who called games for 20 years. In 1964 he also began doing play-by-play for the Cincinnati Reds. Tragically he died of throat cancer in 1967 at the age of 42. Claude was ultimately supplanted as the Voice of the Wildcats by Cawood Ledford, who was then replaced upon his retirement by Ralph Hacker, and Leach followed them.

Leach, from as early as a senior at Bourbon County High School, listed his career choice to be "the next voice of the Wildcats." A 1983

(Note: It's also here you may be able to meet or interact with the Men in Blue, Boogie Guy, the Superfan, the mascots, or even former players or celebrities).

But the point here is to get a seat down as close to Tom Leach, Mike Pratt, and the UK Radio gang as possible. You'll see them sitting down near the scorer's table, wearing headsets and such. The tradition is that the most valuable player, as well as the head coach, will come out after the game for interviews with Leach and Pratt. They graduate of UK, Leach has done well following in those legends' footsteps.

He began his career on the UK Network in 1989, at first hosting the postgame scoreboard and call-in shows. In 1997, Hacker passed on the play-by-play duties for UK football, and in 2001, Leach also assumed the basketball duties. His website, www.tomleachky.com, notes that Leach has been chosen four times as Kentucky Sportscaster of the Year.

Mike Pratt is one of the legends of Kentucky basketball. Pratt played for three years at UK under Adolph Rupp from 1967 to 1970 and scored 1,359 points. As a senior he was named first team All SEC, second team All-American and Academic All-American. After playing for the ABA's Kentucky Colonels he became an assistant at UNC Charlotte and helped lead the 49ers to the Final Four in 1977.

Pratt then became head coach of the team and compiled a 56–52 record over four seasons before being relieved. In 2001 he took over as the color analyst alongside Leach for UK's radio team, and in 2009, he was inducted into the Kentucky Athletic Hall of Fame. To this day, if they're watching games from home, fans will turn down the television broadcast to listen to UK's commentators on the radio. The tradition continues to this day with Tom and Mike. There's even a Sports Sync radio that helps sync up Tom and Mike with the game on television, so you don't have any delay in the play-by-play of the game, available, among other places, at tomleachky.com.

broadcast the interviews over the speakers in the arena so all the fans can listen.

And here's the fun part: most of the time, John Calipari will sign your basketball. Sometimes he'll do a lot of them. Other times he'll only do a few as he may have to leave quickly for a recruiting trip. If you are (or have) a little kid, there's an even better shot at getting it signed. And sometimes—after a really big win—he may even sign all of them.

—Ryan

OTHER FAMOUS EATERIES IN LEXINGTON

So maybe you don't want some great fried chicken brought to your car? Okay—there are other places to chow in the great city of Lexington. We've got steaks, seafood, sushi, Cajun, Japanese, breakfast food, and more. And none of them are far from the basketball arena. We'll talk about a few of the most notable spots later. But consider this the honorable mention section, for a few other great eateries that deserve your consideration.

In random order:

Blue Door Smokehouse: Barbecue, 226 Walton Avenue

Texas barbecue in Kentucky. Brisket, pulled pork, etc. Potato salad and all the fixin's. And a friendly staff to boot.

Coles 735 Main: Japanese, Mediterranean, Vegetarian, 735 East Main Street

Filet mignon, duck breast, scallops, Brussels sprouts and bacon appetizers, desserts, bourbon. What more do you need?

B J Spalding's Bakery: Pastries, doughnuts, desserts, 760 Winchester Road

Everyone says this bakery makes the best doughnuts they've ever had—chocolate, glazed, whatever. Just try them. Especially when they're warm.

Merrick Inn: American, 1074 Merrick Drive

Fried chicken, fish, and more in this old converted farmhouse that has been a Lexington staple for more than 40 years.

Ramsey's Diner: American comfort food, 3090 Helmsdale Place

Hot browns, Reubens, veggie plates—just like Grandma makes.

Bourbon n' Toulouse: Cajun, 829 E Euclid Avenue

Gumbo. Jambalaya. Rice. In Kentucky. Eat it up.

Wild Eggs: Breakfast, 3735 Palomar Center Drive

Try the coffee of the day, or something else—like bagels, salmon, poached eggs, etc. Everything is fresh, and this is the place to be for brunch.

Bella Notte: Italian, 3715 Nicholasville Road

Plentiful pasta portions, a romantic ambiance and great service make this place a can't-miss.

Malone's: Steak, fish, sushi, 1920 Pleasant Ridge Drive

Filets. King crab legs. Oysters on the halfshell. You want it? Malone's has it.

Windy Corner Market: Deli, sandwiches, 4595 Bryan Station Road

Scenic drive to a rustic locale that offers great desserts and views of horse country on all sides.

Saul Good Restaurant and Pub: Burgers, pizza, pork chops, and Martinis, 3801 Nicholasville Road

Folks get things like Black and blue burgers, Argentinian steak pizzas, and Pixy Stix Martinis.

So you've seen a win, possibly gotten your ball signed, and enjoyed the sights and sounds of Rupp Arena. Make sure and listen to the postgame interviews before heading out. The good news is most of the traffic will be gone by this time, making it easy to depart.

But we've got one last recommendation to make on your way home: listen to Matt Jones on the Kentucky Sports Radio postgame call-in show as you head to grab dinner at the Parkette Drive-In. Roll down the windows, turn up 84 WHAS on your radio, and settle in to listen to your fellow fans revel in basketball glory. Maybe you could even call in to the show and let everyone know what good a time you had.

There are many restaurants in Lexington that could provide a superb meal and ambiance at an affordable price. Sit-down places, fancy places, fast food places, and hometown-style places. It all depends on what you want.

Here, we're recommending a place that has been featured on the Food Network and Rachel Ray's talk show. It's a Lexington icon: the **Parkette Drive-In Restaurant**, a carhop where waiters and waitresses bring food out to your car (perfect for listening to the radio while you eat). The Parkette is famous for its fried chicken, burgers, fries, onion rings, and shakes.

"When Joe Smiley opened the Parkette on November 11, 1951, he had a dream. He was a pioneer and visionary in the restaurant industry," the restaurant's website says. "Joe created his own version of the Double-Decker hamburger called the 'Poor Boy.' Joe brought this burger idea with him from West Virginia. He named it after the life that he saw there. Joe said, 'When the coal strikes were on, everybody was starving.'"

Joe then came to Lexington, and even though he saw nothing but dirt roads, he decided the town needed a restaurant. The Parkette was born. In 1953, the restaurant's iconic 40-foot-tall sign was created.

"Joe believed that good food at a good price would bring folks in," the website says. "He was right."

Now, more than 50 years later, the restaurant is still there at 1230 E. New Circle Road. The sign still brings in people from all around, glowing like something out of Las Vegas.

There have been a few changes. When the restaurant was refurbished, the new owners added Chicago-style hot dogs to the menu. But it still features the same affordable prices: burgers under $5, chicken dinners under $8.

Just watch out though—it's closed Sundays.

So there you have it. The perfect game day in Lexington at the University of Kentucky as described by us, your humble tour guides. We hope you've enjoyed yourselves on this trip.

But come on, don't linger behind for too long—there's more you need to see and do as a UK fan.

A lot more. Come this way to see what else lies on the Kentucky Wildcats Fans' Bucket List....

Chapter 2

See Cat City

Just because you've seen a UK basketball game, even if you met all the criteria of the "Ultimate Game Day Experience," doesn't mean you've done all there is to do in Lexington. Heck, we're just getting started. We've got to talk about Keeneland and UK football, about Big Blue Madness, about other places to eat, and so much more. You might be knee deep in Lexington, but if you're going all the way Blue, dive in deeper.

Let's Play Two: Keeneland and UK Football Doubleheader

WHERE: Lexington. Keeneland is at 4201 Versailles Road; Commonwealth Stadium is at 1540 University Drive. The two locations are six miles apart.

WHEN: That's the tricky part. Keeneland's fall meet usually runs from the first Friday in October to the Saturday three weeks later. Whether UK football is at home or is playing a night game is a matter governed almost exclusively by the SEC television situation. Watch carefully and cross your fingers—start times for SEC football games are usually announced 12 days before the Saturday games.

HOW TO DO IT: Head on in. Keeneland isn't hard to visit, and most years and opponents don't render UK football as a terribly difficult ticket.

COST FACTOR: $$ per person. Keeneland charges $5 for general admission for those over 12 (those under are free), while reserved seats are $20 for Saturday meets. UK football tickets vary, but are usually around $50 on the free market. Depending on the quality of opponent and of the ticket, it might be a little higher or lower.

DIFFICULTY FACTOR: ▌ The schedule is the only thing that makes this one tough. You can almost guarantee no more than two chances per year. One is more common, and zero, unfortunately, is not unheard of.

BUCKET RANK: 🗑 🗑 🗑 🗑 🗑

HINTS FOR LITTLE WILDCATS/RELUCTANT WILDCATS:
Keeneland is a Lexington tradition. Some will enjoy the site much more than the sports, some—notably those who don't want to dress up or are uncomfortable with gambling or drinking—won't be as impressed. As an alternative for those who are uncomfortable with Keeneland, the Kentucky Horse Park (4089 Iron Works Parkway, Lexington) is a much more casual, family-friendly destination, and their Christmas light display is a nice late-season treat.

• •

In the lexicon of ultimate Big Blue events, a very close second to the experience of a UK basketball home game is the Keeneland/UK football doubleheader. Keeneland was founded in 1936 as an outgrowth of Kentucky's growing fascination with thoroughbred horses. It was established on a farm owned by Jack Keene, with the twin aims of being a world-class racetrack and a sale facility. It fit the bill on both fronts. A 2009 ranking by the Horseplayers Association of North American ranked Keeneland as the best thoroughbred racetrack in North America.

The track has spring meets in April and fall meets in October. The spring meets catch frequent Kentucky April showers and lack the disadvantage of coinciding with a major sports event. Thus, the fall season is the one to enjoy. As of the 2015 season, the track opens at 11:00 AM daily, with post time for the first race set for 1:05 PM. Races follow approximately every half-hour thereafter. Lawn chairs and umbrellas are permitted; outside alcohol and coolers are not. Dress is relatively formal, with jacket and tie required and denim banned in the clubhouse. Beautiful fall weather, amazing Kentucky thoroughbreds, and a stunning gallery of Lexington's best dressed and most eligible make Keeneland *the* fall hotspot.

Across town on University Drive, under the lights of Commonwealth Stadium, UK Wildcat football faces the grueling foes of the

UK SHINING STARS

UK football may not equal basketball in national success. But the program has seen its share of shining stars. Here's a thumbnail sketch of a few.

Paul "Bear" Bryant had been the head coach at Maryland for one year when he was entrusted with the UK head coaching position in 1946. He stayed in Lexington for eight seasons, compiling a record of 60–23–5. His 1950 Wildcats were 11–1 and upset No. 1 Oklahoma in the 1951 Sugar Bowl. Bryant left UK after 1953 for Texas A&M, but he made his reputation winning national titles at Alabama.

Vito "Babe" Parilli was Bryant's star quarterback. He threw for 4,351 yards and 50 touchdowns from 1949 to 1951, school records that stood for four and a half decades. Parilli led UK to three bowl appearances, including wins in the Sugar and Cotton Bowls. He went on to play 15 years in the AFL and NFL.

Southeastern Conference. The fall Kentucky evenings are perfect football weather, and those who wagered wisely at Keeneland carry a little extra joy into the stadium for football. Kentucky football is often thought of as something of a red-headed stepchild to UK basketball. The program has won only two SEC championships, one in 1950 under then-coach Bear Bryant and a shared title in 1976. But overwhelmingly, the fickle fans who claim to be only fans of UK basketball could only be those who have never enjoyed a game in Commonwealth Stadium.

Art Still was a fearsome defensive end who led the 1976 and 1977 UK teams to national prominence. Behind an All-American career from Still, UK won the 1976 Peach Bowl and went 10–1 in 1977, when they were ineligible for a bowl berth. Still, whose sister Valerie was the greatest UK women's basketball player ever, was chosen with the 2nd overall pick in the 1978 NFL Draft. He played 12 years in the pros, and made the Pro Bowl four times.

Tim Couch was a Kentucky legend from his days at Hyden's Leslie County High, where he set national high school passing records. In 1997 and 1998, Couch threw for almost 8,500 yards and 75 touchdowns at UK. He led the team to the 1999 Outback Bowl and was chosen first overall in that year's NFL Draft. Injuries shortened his pro career, but Couch is currently a TV analyst for Fox Sports.

Randall Cobb was a bit undersized and significantly under-recruited, but became one of the best wide receivers in UK history. Despite playing quarterback before his time at UK, Cobb parlayed his speed, catching ability, and toughness into a UK-record 37 touchdowns scored. A second-round NFL Draft choice of the Green Bay Packers in 2011, Cobb has become an All-Pro NFL pick.

I saw my first home game on a fall night in 1994. Kentucky went 1–10 in that difficult season, but sitting in Commonwealth Stadium on a comfortable fall evening and watching UK star running back Moe Williams try to outduel the South Carolina Gamecocks convinced me that this was how truly civilized people spent their time. With the addition of years, I realize I was half right. Those in the know hit Keeneland first, for that ultimate Bluegrass doubleheader. The football game may be won or lost, but the memories are always sweet regardless.

—Joe

Attend the Cat Walk

WHERE: Outside Commonwealth Stadium, at the Corner of Jerry Claiborne Way and College Way in front of Nutter Field House; the players enter the stadium through Gate 1.

WHEN: Generally, two hours and fifteen minutes prior to kickoff for home football games

HOW TO DO IT: Hang around and cheer for the Wildcats

COST FACTOR: Free

DIFFICULTY FACTOR: ▮ Might want to arrive a little early for a good spot, but adverse weather aside, this couldn't be easier.

BUCKET RANK: 🗑 🗑 🗑

HINTS FOR LITTLE WILDCATS/RELUCTANT WILDCATS: It's an easy chance to get up close with UK football players and coaches.

B ecause football is a game of violence, in which giant, speedy behemoths try to tear each other's heads off for four quarters, it is a pretty integral part of the entire process for the Wildcat football team to get a little bit pumped up. Enter the fan base.

On game days, the Wildcat team—players and coaches—stroll into Commonwealth Stadium in the Cat Walk. It's a leisurely event, with the players dressed up in business attire, but ready to start psyching themselves up for football with hometown cheers and congratulations.

EXTRA POINTS

Memorable UK Football Moments

While UK football can't claim a history as distinguished as Wildcat basketball, there have been a host of memorable UK football moments. Here are a handful of the biggest:

- January 1, 1951: UK 13, Oklahoma 7 (1951 Sugar Bowl). Coach Paul "Bear" Bryant's Wildcats were 10–1 entering the game, but seemed outmatched by the top-ranked Sooners, who held a 31-game winning streak. Led by some timely defense and efficient offense, UK took a 13–0 halftime lead, and held on to shock the nation with what may be the program's biggest victory.

- September 26, 1964: UK 27, Ole Miss 21. Coach Charlie Bradshaw's Wildcats, led by All-American receiver Rick Kestner, upset top-ranked Ole Miss at Jackson, Mississippi. While the team ended up going 5–5 that year, the upset was a classic.

- November 20, 1976: UK 7, Tennessee 0. On a cold day in Knoxville, UK ended the regular season by beating UT courtesy of a pass from quarterback Derrick Ramsey to running back Greg Woods. The game clinched a share of the SEC title for the Cats.

- October 1, 1977: UK 24, Penn State 20. The Wildcats, en route to a 10–1 campaign, shocked Joe Paterno's Nittany Lions in Happy Valley.

- October 4, 1997: UK 40, Alabama 34 (OT). Under first-year coach Hal Mumme, Kentucky won only its second game ever over Alabama, as star QB Tim Couch hit wide receiver Craig Yeast with the game-winning score in UK's first-ever overtime game.

- October 13, 2007: UK 43, LSU 37 (3 OT). With CBS broadcasting the game nationally, UK went toe-to-toe with the top-ranked LSU Tigers and won. Quarterback Andre Woodson was superb, and wide receiver Stevie Johnson caught the winning score. LSU was unfazed, as they went on to win the national title.

One of the best perks of the Cat Walk is a chance to realize just how imposing the Wildcats can be. UK defensive end Za'Darius Smith, for instance, was always immaculately dressed, and sometimes was joined by his young daughter in the Cat Walk. But his stylish wardrobe and genteel expression did nothing to offset the fact that in the course of one handshake, a typical fan realizes that Smith's hands literally swallow his or her hands, and that at 6'6", 260 pounds, whatever the fabric that Smith is built from simply can't be the same materials of which normal people consist.

Aside from the home-game Cat Walks, UK often organizes the event on the road. For instance, the 2006 Music City Bowl experience began with a raucous Cat Walk outside LP Field in Nashville. UK jumped to a 28–6 lead, largely off of the emotion that the team experienced. UK defensive coordinator Mike Archer commented in the season-highlight film, *Believe*, "All of the people there for Wildcat Walk, I've never seen anything like it in my life. That had a very positive impact on our players. As we took the long walk down into the tunnel that was all they were talking about." Buoyed by the fan support, UK pulled off a 28–20 upset win over Clemson.

After that particular game, all of Big Blue Nation was elated. Selfies were taken, phone calls were made, and a bowl trophy was hoisted. But it was the hearty souls who made it in early, who motivated the Cats through the Cat Walk, who might have been the real MVPs. If the football Wildcats can ever again successfully change the game and compete in the SEC, it might well begin in the Cat Walk.

Homecoming at UK

WHERE: Lexington, ultimately centering around Commonwealth Stadium at 1540 University Drive

WHEN: While the schedule varies based on television and the balancing of home and away football games, homecoming is in October, usually for a night game.

HOW TO DO IT: There are plenty of free or cheap events. For the most part, show up.

COST FACTOR: $$ per person for the football tickets. Most of the rest is cheap or free.

DIFFICULTY FACTOR: ▌ Not very

BUCKET RANK: 🗑 🗑 🗑 🗑

HINTS FOR LITTLE WILDCATS/RELUCTANT WILDCATS:
Parades, carnivals, etc. There's something for everybody.

O ne hundred years ago, some wise Wildcat got the bright idea of having an annual weekend to bring back friends and alumni, center the event around a football game, and enjoy a homecoming event. Kentucky beat Tennessee 6–0 in the first homecoming football game on November 25, 1915, and a tradition was born.

While the exact records are unclear, it is certain that every football season since World War II ended has featured a homecoming game, with attendant festivities. A parade of student floats, a homecoming court, and a raucous tailgating scene make Homecoming Saturday *the*

HOMECOMING HIGHLIGHTS

A few previous homecoming highlights:

1973: In the first homecoming game in Commonwealth Stadium, a 3–4 UK team crushed No. 14 Tulane 34–7, as UK's Sonny Collins ran for 176 yards and three touchdowns. UK won its first eight homecoming games in the new stadium.

1983: Coming off 1982's 0–10–1 record, second-year coach Jerry Claiborne and his Cats beat Tulane 26–14, moving to 4–0 on the season. UK went on to post a 6–4–1 regular season record and appeared in the Hall of Fame Bowl.

1991: Kentucky's streak of eight consecutive homecoming wins seemed likely to end in a tie, but on the final play of the game, UK's Doug Pelfrey (whose girlfriend had been named homecoming queen) nailed a 53-yard field goal to beat Cincinnati 20–17.

2006: Rich Brooks' UK team scored a major homecoming upset, knocking off Georgia 24–20. Kentucky was on its way to its first eight-win season since 1984, and fans stormed the field, tearing up the goalposts on this memorable homecoming.

2008: Trailing 20–7 late in the 4th quarter, Kentucky rallied on a pair of late touchdown passes to Randall Cobb to stun Bobby Petrino and Arkansas by a 21–20 count. The win enabled Kentucky to appear in— and win—its third consecutive bowl game.

A cautionary word—all homecoming days aren't golden. Likely my most memorable UK homecoming game was a 31–14 loss in the rain to Mississippi State in 2007, capping a day in which I, likely due to the influence of pain medication following wisdom teeth removal, managed at one point to hop out of my car while the vehicle was in football game of the year to enjoy. It probably doesn't hurt that the Wildcats are 46–22 in the game since World War II.

If you speak with a dozen different UK alums, you'll probably learn about a dozen different homecoming-week traditions. The parade is an old-time favorite, complete with floats from various student organizations and the UK marching band, that took on new life with its move to downtown Lexington—which does aid with parking and dining options for those who don't reside on campus. The Kitty Karnival is an evening of fun for the youngest Wildcats, with activities ranging from face painting to a petting zoo. A Homecoming Street Fair was introduced in 2014 on the Avenue of Champions, and a reunion for the 50th-anniversary graduates always draws an enthusiastic crowd.

But this is a book about sports, after all, and homecoming football is always exciting. While Commonwealth Stadium is usually mostly full regardless of the quality of opponent, the bleachers will be crammed full on homecoming night. Kentucky's fans, perhaps enjoying the fall weather, perhaps buoyed by an evening of socializing, or perhaps just thirsty to kick some butt, are behind their team with all of their might.

And for some, homecoming is extra special. In 2000, Kentucky place kicker Seth Hanson held his usual starting role—even making a 36-yard field goal in the game. He also was awarded the title of homecoming king at halftime. Anything can—and will—probably happen at homecoming. And it's sure to be a good time.

Check Out the Blue-White Game (Basketball) or Spring Game (Football)

WHERE: Rupp Arena (used to be in Memorial Coliseum, but not in the last few years) and Commonwealth Stadium

WHEN: Blue-White game(s) are in late October or early November, and the Spring Game (except in 2015, when stadium construction prevented it from occurring) is on a Saturday in late April.

HOW TO DO IT: Tickets are sold online, although there is a healthy resale market as well.

COST FACTOR: $ For once, for a UK game, it's pretty much a steal. Spring Game tickets are usually free, although there may be a small convenience charge (approximately $5) on the purchase. Blue-White tickets have recently been $5 in the lower deck and $10 in the upper deck.

DIFFICULTY FACTOR: ▮ Trust me. I (Joe) sat on the 50-yard line in the second row and watched Tim Couch play in the Spring Game. Seat quality has declined a bit as interest has increased, but for once the usual suspects aren't nabbing all the good seats.

BUCKET RANK: 🗑 🗑 🗑 🗑 🗑

HINTS FOR LITTLE WILDCATS/RELUCTANT WILDCATS: Fan Day (which comes in early August every football season) might be a better choice, because you can watch a little football and then nab autographs or take pictures with players or coaches. But the activities listed on this page feature all the fun of game day with none of the stress or expense.

Can't get into a UK game at Rupp Arena? Maybe you can see your favorite stars, like Karl-Anthony Towns, during a Blue-White preseason scrimmage. (Tim Sofranko)

If you've spent the last few years wondering which horse-farming family you'd have to marry into to sit on the 50-yard line or in the first few rows at Rupp Arena, there is hope...well, outside of impending matrimony. The annual Blue-White game(s) and football Spring Game give you a chance at a prime seat and a chance to watch your favorite Cats in action—without much expense or haggling.

Whether it's a chance to see the backup quarterbacks in action, or to see Kentucky play some real competition in basketball early in the season (and come on, an intrasquad scrimmage in recent years has been much more competitive than the team's exhibition games against University of Pikeville or Transylvania), the Spring Game and Blue-White game are the best bang for your buck in Wildcat land.

Here are a few recent highlights from each game:

Blue-White Game

- In 1999, Jamaal Magloire scored 33 points in the game, leading Blue to a hard-fought win over White.

- Three days before Halloween 2009, John Calipari's Cats had their first public battle in the Blue-White game. The stars that night range from memorable (25 points for John Wall) to predictable (24 points for Patrick Patterson) to totally random (24 points for Darnell Dodson).

- In 2010, Brandon Knight had 37 points to lead all scorers. But perhaps more important, Josh Harrellson posted 10 points and 16 rebounds for the losing White squad. After the game, Calipari commented on how concerned he was with the rebounding...and Harrellson took to Twitter to complain about the lack of praise. Harrellson was disciplined, and subsequently proved to Calipari and Big Blue Nation with an astonishing senior season that the scrimmage wasn't a fluke.

Blue-White Games in the Lost Season

Due to NCAA probation, Adolph Rupp's Wildcats did not play a schedule in 1952–53. However, the great coach was never one to lose time, so he arranged a series of four scrimmages during the '52–'53 season. Rupp varied the setup—one game was freshmen vs. varsity, two others were Frank Ramsey's squad versus Cliff Hagan's, and the final game was a traditional Blue-White matchup. The games were well attended, with at least one cracking the 10,000 mark for attendance in the almost-brand-new Memorial Coliseum.

The real winners were Kentucky fans, who got to see their players, and the Kentucky team, which came back from probation in the 1953–54 season by posting an undefeated regular season.

- The 2011 Blue-White game was the Terrence Jones show. The sophomore scored 52 points, and added 16 rebounds and six assists. Anthony Davis had 27 points and 13 rebounds in a defeat.

Spring Game

- The game stats appear to have been lost to time, but Tim Couch threw for well over 500 yards in the 1998 spring game.

- In 2013, new head coach Mark Stoops's first spring game drew a UK-record crowd of 50,831. The game was a 24–23 contest, with White missing a two-point conversation that would have given them the lead in the closing minutes.

- In 2014, UK quarterback Patrick Towles showed that he had a leg up in the team's quarterback competition, going 9–for–10 for 110 yards for the Blue team, which won 38–14.

See a UK Hoops (Women's) Basketball Game at Memorial Coliseum

WHERE: Memorial Coliseum, 201 Avenue of Champions, Lexington, Kentucky

WHEN: November through March

HOW TO DO IT: Games are well attended (the team was ninth in the country in national attendance last season) but tickets are easy to come by. Visit http://www.ukathletics.com/tickets/tickets-w-baskbl.html or call (800) 928-2287 for more information.

COST FACTOR: $ to $$ This is an inexpensive way to watch great basketball. $9 for reserved seats and $5 for children and seniors. Kids under 5 are *free*. And parking is *free*, too.

DIFFICULTY FACTOR: ▌ This is a great experience. Three parking garages offer free parking and shuttles running to the coliseum.

BUCKET RANK: 🗑 🗑 🗑 🗑

HINTS FOR LITTLE WILDCATS/RELUCTANT WILDCATS: A great environment for children and nonfans. These women play a style that is frenetic and fun to watch—lots of forced turnovers, lots of running up and down the court, lots of pressure defense, and lots of three-point shooting. It's not unusual for coaches and players to come out after the game and interact with fans and children. You can even host a child's birthday party here.

After serving as the men's basketball home for 25 years, the women's basketball squad took over as tenants of Memorial Coliseum in the mid-1970s. (Ryan Clark)

For the last decade, UK Hoops (also known as the UK women's basketball program) has annually cracked the top 10 to become one of the nation's most successful women's programs. Head coach Matthew Mitchell has led his team to three Elite Eight finishes in the NCAA Tournament in the last six years while winning an SEC Championship and producing two SEC Players of the Year.

But what could be even more remarkable his how marketable he has made the UK Hoops team. Women's basketball games are now an event on campus. This, of course, has led to a boom in recruiting. (For the first time ever, UK started three McDonald's All-Americans on its team). Mitchell has provided a great face for the program. After stints as an assistant under Pat Summit at Tennessee and at Florida, Mitchell coached at Morehead State for two seasons before coming to UK.

He quickly caught on with players and fans. Anyone who has watched his coach's show (where he frequently plays guitar and sings), seen one of his dances at Big Blue Madness (he has impersonated James Brown and Bruno Mars, among others), or listened to him as a fill-in host for Kentucky Sports Radio (his pseudo-feud with guest host Ryan Lemond is legendary) knows the man has personality—and he is not afraid to show it. It's no wonder then why his players, and the community, love him. Of course, anyone can love a man with personality. The thing is, he and his team have made UK Hoops fun to *watch*.

"He's become an ambassador for this university in some very, very unique ways," Kentucky Athletics Director Mitch Barnhart told the *Lexington Herald-Leader* in 2012.

"He's the type guy who feels like he's never gone to work a day in his life because he loves what he does," Mark Hudspeth, coach at Louisiana-Lafayette, told the *Herald-Leader*. Hudspeth grew up with Mitchell in Louisville, Mississippi. "He's never been a coach that looks for his next opportunity. They always seem to find him."

These women play hard for Mitchell. They are talented, and their style of play is intoxicating. They shoot a lot of threes. They play frenetic defense. And you get the feeling they would run through a wall for their coach. It all adds up to a big bucket-list opportunity: You have to see these women play in Memorial Coliseum.

Located just around the back from the Craft Center stands Memorial Coliseum, the 10,000-seat venue where UK Hoops hosts its games. The facility opened in 1950 and also hosts UK's volleyball and gymnastics squads. On the walls you'll see (like Rupp Arena) more banners of historical accomplishments—and the UK Hoops accomplishments are growing, just like their audience.

UK Hoops games are a family affair (you'll regularly see Coach Mitchell's wife and kids at games, as well as parents and siblings of the

EXTRA POINTS

Three of the Best from Matthew Mitchell's Tenure

There have been a number of truly remarkable games in Matthew Mitchell's brief tenure. There was the four-overtime game where No. 5 Kentucky defeated No. 9 Baylor in Arlington, 133–130 (UK guard Jennifer O'Neill scored a school-record 43 points in that game—*coming off the bench*), but that didn't occur in Memorial Coliseum. Here are three huge victories/series for UK Hoops during Mitchell's tenure:

1. **2011–15**: In what has become a heated rivalry in its own right, Kentucky has defeated Louisville four consecutive times over the past four seasons, and the game always seems to come down to the last bucket. In December 2013, UK trumped Louisville 69–64 in a filled Memorial Coliseum.

2. **March 1, 2015**: South Carolina came into Memorial Coliseum ranked No. 2 in the country with one loss on the season—to No. 1 Connecticut. The Gamecocks were also undefeated at 15–0 in the SEC. They ran into a buzzsaw in No. 13 Kentucky, as Jennifer O'Neill and Makayla Epps combined for 22 second-half points and UK made 27 of 35 free throws in a 67–56 victory.

3. **January 12, 2012**: A'dia Mathies scored 34 points and hit the game-winner as No. 9 Kentucky beat No. 6 Tennessee 61–60.

players). And besides the girl power, the positive vibes, and the low prices, there are other reasons to see a UK Hoops game at Memorial Coliseum:

- Watch for former and current athletes to attend, too. Many times you'll be able to see the men's basketball squad showing up to support the ladies, or you'll see famous female alums (like perhaps Valerie Still, who is still the Queen of All Women's Basketball at UK. In four years in the early 80s she scored more points than any other player—man or woman—at UK: 2,763, before playing for the Washington Mystics of the WNBA).

- If Rupp Arena has its ice cream, then Memorial Coliseum has its kettle corn. You must have some while you're there.

- After each game, the whole team, Coach Mitchell, and probably his wife and kids will all lead the crowd in singing "On, On, U of K." It's a blast to watch—and even more fun to participate in.

So bring the family—at a UK Hoops game, you'll more than likely find a bigger one to join. As we said, there's a good chance the players and coach may come out and greet the crowd. That can especially happen if you wait around long enough.

—Ryan

Go Beyond the Usual Suspects (Basketball and Football)

When you think of the Kentucky Wildcats, you probably think of basketball, and of Rupp Arena, and Coach Calipari. Or maybe you think of Coach Stoops and a Keeneland/Commonwealth Stadium doubleheader. Or maybe Coach Mitchell and his scrappy, blood-in-their-eyes hoops team spring to mind. But there are so many more treats for the serious Cat backer. Don't take our word—get out there and watch. A few of the most notable "other" Wildcat squads (other than cheerleading, which is covered elsewhere in this book):

Softball: Coach Rachel Lawson led UK to the program's first College World Series appearance in 2014. John Cropp Stadium is a first-rate facility, and enabled UK to host the 2013 SEC Tournament.

Baseball: Star first baseman/pitcher and consensus Player of the Year A.J. Reed has departed Lexington, but the Bat Cats are on a solid run under coach Gary Henderson. In 2012, Henderson's squad was No. 1 in the nation at one point, and they ran off a 22-game winning streak en route to the best NCAA finish in team history. Cliff Hagan Stadium has been renovated three times, and with a 3,000 seating capacity, it's a cozy place to enjoy a game.

Men's Tennis: Former All-American Cedric Kauffman always leads a competitive squad, and last year's team reached the NCAA Sweet 16.

Rifle: UK won a rifle national championship in 2011, and Wildcat Connor Davis won a national title in air rifle in 2014.

REMEMBER "WAH WAH" JONES

Who: The greatest multisport athlete in UK history

Why: If you played a sport, he was better at it than you were. Whatever the sport was…literally

Where to Find Jones: Sadly, he passed away in 2014. But read up. He's got quite a story.

If there ever has truly been a Wildcat for all seasons, Wallace "Wah Wah" Jones was the man. A native of Harlan, Kentucky, Jones grew up excelling in pretty much every sport—and he never stopped. After Adolph Rupp won a recruiting battle over Tennessee, Jones was a three-time All-American as a basketball player, and was a part of two NCAA championship teams.

That said, while the other players rested and caught up on their homework, Jones also was an All-SEC wide receiver under football coach Paul "Bear" Bryant. He helped UK to its first ever bowl win in 1947. He also moonlighted in baseball, playing the game at a sufficient level that he was offered a contract by the major league Boston Braves.

Jones briefly played in the NBA, before moving back to Kentucky. At the age of 27, he was elected sheriff of Fayette County. He became a successful businessman, and was the last survivor of Kentucky basketball's famous Fabulous Five when he passed away in 2014.

Golf: Pros like Gay Brewer and J.B. Holmes are Wildcat golf alums, and the squad finished in the top ten in the NCAA three consecutive years in the 2000s.

Volleyball: Coach Craig Skinner has racked up a fair amount of success in Lexington, with his team going to ten straight NCAA Tournaments.

Soccer: Just one note here…when you cheer for the Soccer Cats, don't break out the familiar "S-E-C" chant. As UK and South Carolina are the only traditional SEC schools that have incorporated men's soccer as a varsity sport, the Cats are actually a member of CUSA in soccer (as are the Gamecocks). Soccer has made five NCAA Tournament appearances and the Cats won four conference championships in the early 2000s, at that time in the Mid-American Conference (MAC).

EXTRA POINTS

UK Athletics Director Mitch Barnhart

Largely based on the success of these teams, UK athletics director Mitch Barnhart capped off an amazing run in 2015 by being named Under Armour's Athletics Director of the Year.

"Under the steady and successful leadership of Mitch Barnhart, the University of Kentucky athletics program is reaching extraordinary levels of success across its 22 varsity programs," said President Eli Capilouto. "For 13 years, his integrity and talent have empowered our staff, coaches and student-athletes to succeed on the field, in the classroom and across the communities they serve."

In 2015, UK completed Barnhart's 15 by 15 by 15 Plan, set in 2008, which required UK athletics to win 15 conference or national titles by the year 2015. In the 2013–14 school year, UK finished 11th in NACDA Directors' Cup standings, meeting Barnhart's aim to make Kentucky a top-15 athletics department nationally. UK also has reached the academic prong of 15 by 15 by 15 in five consecutive semesters by achieving a department-wide grade-point average of 3.0 or better.

Track and Field: The 2015 season was also a banner year for the Kentucky women's track and field team, which finished as the National Runner-Up, the program's best-ever finish, at the 2015 NCAA Outdoor Championships at the University of Oregon. "It was a group effort," third-year head coach Edrick Floreal said. "Now we have to find a way to get the (first-place) trophy." Floreal, who came to Kentucky from Stanford, is quickly building a track and field powerhouse in Lexington. Seniors Kendra Harrison and Dezerea Bryant, the duo responsible for helping turn the Wildcats into a national track and field power, led UK in the championships, with each turning in her best performance as a collegiate competitor. And Harrison went on to be named National Track Athlete of the Year.

Gymnastics: Kentucky has long been known as a competitor on the national stage in gymnastics. In 2015, UK freshman Sydney Waltz qualified for the NCAA Championships, becoming the 11th Wildcat in program history to do so. She is the first to earn an all-around bid since Aronda Primault in 2002. But it all started with Jenny Hansen back in the early 1990s. How's this for a resume: eight NCAA gymnastics championship titles; a record three-straight all-around titles from 1993 to 1995; thirteen All-America honors; Kentucky Sportsman of the Year in 1995; most outstanding gymnast of the past 25 years as recognized by the NCAA. "Simply put," one ukathletics. com blog post put it, "she's still the greatest gymnast in program history and one of the best student-athletes to don UK's colors."

Attend Big Blue Madness!

WHERE: Rupp Arena

WHEN: Late October, not long before the basketball season begins

HOW TO DO IT: You can get on the Internet. Or you can camp out for tickets.

COST FACTOR: $ Not a lot. For the Internet, you have to pay a charge: $5. To camp out, you have to have supplies—blankets, tents, etc. But ultimately, the tickets are free.

DIFFICULTY FACTOR: ▌ It's difficult sometimes because everyone logs on to the Internet at once, so you have to know what you're doing. As for camping out, between the time commitment, battling the elements, knowing the right people to navigate the situation, etc., this is a tough one. Plus, you'll either have to be a college student, or you'll have to take a week off of work to do this. But don't laugh—people do it that way every year.

BUCKET RANK: 🗑️ 🗑️ 🗑️ 🗑️ 🗑️

HINTS FOR LITTLE WILDCATS/RELUCTANT WILDCATS: In terms of an event, Big Blue Madness is made for young ones. There's lots of music and even some fireworks (which can be loud, so be careful of that) but overall, you always see lots of kids. In terms of camping out, there's a lot of downtime involved—and a lot of waiting. And when the UK folks tell you it's time to run across the street for your spot, it's a free-for-all where some folks have gotten hurt. This is not the environment for little kids. Bring them to Big Blue Madness—but leave them at home if you're camping out, waiting for tickets.

Few events are more exciting, and more fan friendly, than Big Blue Madness. Every year, when the season winds down with an exciting (or disappointing) finish, the calendar flips, and fans start counting down the days to the next Big Blue Madness.

"In 1982, Joe B. Hall was in search of a way to promote his team with some preseason excitement," wrote Hayes Gardner for the *Kentucky Kernel* newspaper. "His idea: to hold a practice open to the public at midnight the day of the first team practice. At 12:01 AM, the 'Midnight Special' became a reality as 8,500 spectators filed into Memorial Coliseum to get a first glimpse of their Cats. The 12,000-seat auditorium had thousands of vacant seats, though."

That's right—it's a practice. We're talking about a practice (hat tip to Allen Iverson). But seriously, this is a showcase. Most of the time there are dunk contests and shooting contests, along with a scrimmage, cheerleaders, speeches, and a lot of excitement.

And it's free. It's the official kickoff to the basketball season.

Hall reportedly got the idea from Lefty Driesell, who is credited with conducting the first Midnight Madness when he was the head coach at Maryland in 1971.

Gardner, of the *Kernel*, reported that a lot of the local media didn't even cover UK's first event.

"To be honest, I don't remember much about the first couple years of Big Blue Madness," said UK alumna Liz Bryant.

Over the years, however, the event transformed. For one, it's gotten bigger. Routinely, every media outlet in the state comes to cover the spectacle. We've seen coaches ride out on motorcycles. We've seen players swing down from the rafters dressed as "Cat-man and Robin." We've seen fireworks and athletes come out like they were professional wrestlers.

And, of course, we've seen them all dance.

In 1990, fans started lining up that morning to get tickets. A year later, they were waiting for up to 36 hours in advance. In 1993, fans waited for up to three days to get inside. By 1994, the father-and-son combination of Robert and Ronald Vallandingham of Smithland, Kentucky, arrived on October 10 a full five days early.

That's when things got crazy. In 1995, Wally Clark of Lexington said he would be first in line—so he showed up 17 days early. A year later, he showed up 38 days before Big Blue Madness.

By 2000, tickets started being distributed on the Internet. In 2002, UK celebrated 100 years of basketball. A giant cake was wheeled out to center court at Madness, and Bill Keightley jumped out of it to thunderous applause.

In 2005, Rupp Arena took over as host of Big Blue Madness, and 23,174 spectators came to watch.

And in 2009, John Calipari began what would be a series of presidential-like speeches to the Big Blue Nation about why Kentucky was everything in college basketball.

Over the ensuing years it has become more fashionable for students (and other fans, too) to camp out for days before tickets are released. In 2009, there were more than 500 tents set up. A year later, there were nearly 600. But, if you're like a normal fan, you'll probably want to just try your luck on the Internet.

Here are some tips to getting tickets for Madness on the Internet:

- Have a good, fast Internet connection.

- Have the most updated browser. It makes a difference. You may not see all the options or tasks if you don't.

- Make sure you already have an account on Ticketmaster.com (set up with your credit card and a username, etc.) It will save you time.

- Be at the computer right when the clock hits the time the tickets are distributed (typically 7:00 or 8:00 AM, depending on your time zone).

- As soon as they are distributed, click on the buy button. If it doesn't let you through, keep refreshing it and clicking buy until you get in.

- Remember: you will only be charged a service fee for your ticket. Typically, that's $5 per ticket.

- Do not be greedy. You will probably be able to go for four (or maybe even more) tickets at a time, but because of the number of folks online, and the speed the tickets get gobbled up, just go for two. You'll probably get better seats that way.

- Another way to not be greedy: If you get through, and you get tickets, go ahead and buy them. Do not reject them and try again (which is an option you'll have). Just feel lucky you got through.

- When finished, you can choose how you want your tickets delivered to you.

Of course, as we've said, there are other ways to get tickets, too. There's always eBay, Craigslist, or one of the ticket sites like Guy on the Corner Tickets.

Or...you could camp out.

Camp Out for Big Blue Madness Tickets

Emily Kessinger graduated from the University of Kentucky in December 2014 with a degree in social work. She says she's getting ready to move to Atlanta for a job and she'll probably start graduate school soon, too.

Yet among all of her accomplishments, there is one that she holds closest to her big blue heart.

"My senior year I was the fifth person in line for Big Blue Madness," says the 22-year-old from Hodgenville, Kentucky. "I ended up getting third row, center tickets. It was the coolest thing."

So how does one go about getting such good seats? You need supplies, friends, luck, and experience, Emily says. Of course, she camped out for a week to start.

"I picked a perfect time to come here," Emily says of UK. The Wildcats won a national championship when she was a freshman. That just made her even more of a fan.

As a little girl, her father took her to Big Blue Madness. When she grew up and became a student, she became determined to repay him. As a freshman and sophomore, she camped out, and she got tickets, which was cool, but she also learned.

You want to start paying attention around August, and the media will let you know when tickets will be distributed—normally about a month before Madness, she says.

Each person gets four tickets. That means you can bring friends and help rotate in and out, each watching the tents for a while. "Then you can go to class," Emily says, laughing. Her group had eight people responsible for two tents.

They stocked them with blankets and other items, in case it rained—which it did one year. "And it can get cold," she says. "You're just trying to pass the time. You play cornhole. You do homework. We used to take a generator out there and hook up a TV so we could watch and play video games. But they don't let us take a generator anymore."

For a week, Emily's crew camped out just across the street from Memorial Coliseum. They were surrounded by others doing the same thing. The squatters call themselves "Tent City." One night, Coach Calipari and the players brought pizzas for everyone. On another morning, players brought breakfast.

"One morning I remember Michael Kidd-Gilchrist gave me a sausage biscuit from McDonald's," Emily says. "That was the best breakfast sandwich I've ever eaten."

And as you wait, you become friends, Emily says.

"We've had a great group of people who have waited with us," she says. "There were people who helped us set up our tents and were just really nice."

But there are unwritten rules. "Do not show up later than everyone else and try to get in front," Emily says. "That's a good way to get hurt, because a lot of people will get mad."

After waiting on the other side of the street for a few days, a UK official will come over in the middle of the week and tell everyone to run across the street to get a line in front of Memorial. This can be crazy, Emily says, though UK has made it to where it is done in a more orderly fashion. Then, on Friday, fans are given "control cards" that say what place in line you're in.

"There were four people in line in front of me, so I got number five," Emily says. "So I knew my tickets would be good."

Third row, center court.

"You've got to get here early, get a large group of people to help you, and make sure and talk to those who have done it before," she says. "If you don't you'll regret it. It's probably in the top five things you need to do as a fan."

. . . .

Have an Ultimate Kentucky Weekend

For the creatively inclined looking for a challenge, there's the Ultimate Kentucky Weekend.

Joe Cox and I have done this for a few years, but the thing is, you never know what you're going to get. You could see the football Cats beat a No. 1 team, or you could see them lose to Vandy in horrifically cold weather. We've done both. The only good thing about it was that Commonwealth Stadium was selling hot chocolate and Fazoli's breadsticks. Those were good, at least.

You could see the basketball team kick off a new era with optimism and a new coach, or you could see them lose to Virginia Military Institute, even while Jodie Meeks scored 39.

Again, we've seen that too.

But whenever we can, Joe and I try to take in a football game, or basketball game, that then leads to another on back-to-back days in a weekend. For a long while, that happened to be watching Big Blue Madness, then taking in a football game the next day. The point is we've definitely had some great memories doing this.

The second best would have to be October 2007. (And really, there's only one reason why this isn't No. 1 on the list, and his name is Billy Gillispie.) Joe and I sat for the Big Blue Madness that introduced us to a new coach. He was from Texas. He had just beaten Louisville in the NCAA Tournament. He talked like a southerner. Kind of. The fans were excited. People in the media seemed to think he was the right man for the job.

His name was Billy Gillispie. I had not yet begun writing my fan blog for the *Cincinnati Enquirer* newspaper, so I have no record of exactly what I thought of the moment. But I remember this: I was hopeful. I loved Tubby Smith, but I also realized he may have been tired of the pressures of the UK job. I was ready to embrace a new coach, one who I hoped could get us back to the Final Four.

So I hoped he was the guy. We would later find out that he would not be the guy, but there was so much hope in that arena, it was a good time. And it was followed up by one of the greatest wins in UK football history. That Saturday, Andre Woodson and Kentucky defeated No. 1 LSU in three overtimes. I've never seen anything like it, and I probably never will again. But it wasn't the best Ultimate Kentucky Weekend ever.

The best would have to be October 2010. UK was back to being a contender in basketball. They'd had the most talented team the previous season, and came within one poor performance of the Final Four. Big Blue Madness that year was rockin'.

By that point I was covering these events in my fan blog for the *Enquirer*, so I can go back and look at some of the things I'd written. Here's my take on that Madness:

> It seems like a lot of the extra stuff they normally feature was stripped away in an attempt to just feature the teams. And for this year, both the men and women will be very highly ranked. Some amazing moments:

1. Matthew Mitchell dances with his ladies. YouTube this now if you haven't seen it. I would love to play for a coach like this. You can see why his team loves him.

2. Enes Kanter enters UK lore as the Undertaker. His entrance, complete with hat, rivals anything I've ever seen at Madness. It was hilarious and amazing and as he slowly walked down the platform with fireworks going off, I couldn't help but think how cool it all looked. I really hope this kid gets to play at some point. He's hilarious.

3. Harrellson does the Carlton. Practically dared by the UK fanbase to do this dance, Josh Harrellson comes through to the crowd's delight.

EXTRA POINTS

Now Visit the Wildcats' True Home

Make a trip to Frankfort to see actual wildcats (which are really bobcats) that live in a compound at the Salato Wildlife Education Center.

"Also known as a bay lynx, catamount, or wildcat, bobcats are nocturnal and very shy, but they are extremely effective predators, able to jump eight feet high and 12 feet across to catch their prey," says the Kentucky Department of Fish & Wildlife Resources website. "Their favorite meal? Small mammals like the cottontail rabbit. Though they may look and act like overgrown house cats, they're not!"

But they do make for some great pictures.

Contact:
1 Sportsman's Lane, Frankfort, KY, 40601
(502) 564-7863
or http://fw.ky.gov/Education/Pages/Salato-Wildlife-Education-Center.aspx

4. Knight dunks over Harrelson. We already know this team is going to be long and athletic based on their performance in Canada. I remember last year I'd never seen any college player dunk like Wall or like Bledsoe—and I was so excited to see them get on the court. Knight had two dunks that showed his athleticism and they brought me out of my seat. One in particular over Josh Harrelson was especially sick, as Knight seemed to jump up and over the 6–10 center.

5. Last year's stars talk to the crowd. All of the drafted players from last year's team videotaped messages for the crowd, with the loudest cheers reserved for Patterson, Cousins, and Wall. Each described how they wished they were back in blue, but all were excited about the upcoming NBA season.

And then, of course, there was that football game. Coming in, we really had no idea if we could win. Our football Cats had been a bit bipolar. We could have an explosive offense, but could we put it all together? We faced Spurrier and his South Carolina Gamecocks. They were good (ranked No. 11) but they weren't great. Then again, no UK team had *ever* beaten Spurrier at Florida or South Carolina.

Kentucky promptly came out and found itself down 28–10. Here's what I wrote of that game:

I'll admit that at 28–10 at halftime (when the score could've easily been much worse) my friend Joe and I were debating how high the score would have to get before we actually left. I think if South Carolina would have scored another touchdown and made it 35–10 we would have headed for the exits. But as the story goes, UK held the Gamecocks scoreless for the second half and we remained in our seats to see what may be one of the two best UK wins in the last 20 years.

And along the way, I fell in love with this team all over again. When Mike Hartline (an amazing effort that will be forever remembered by UK fans) lofted the fourth-and-7 pass to a wide-open Randall Cobb for the touchdown, I decided that no matter what—even if the Gamecocks came back to force overtime and win the game—I was so impressed by UK's grit that I was back. This team deserved it. And they deserved a win over Spurrier, who knew how tough this game could be.

So many times UK had come so close, you figured one of these days we had to get lucky and pull it off, right? Well, it wasn't luck. It was Hartline and Cobb and Chris Matthews and an inspired defense that yes, took advantage of a break (the injury to Carolina's running back). But they had to make the plays, and they did and it was amazing.

Now you have to look at the rest of the schedule and see there are still a lot of winnable games out there. At worst, this team should be 6–6. At best? Well, who knows?

Amazing job to the team. Thanks for giving me another great memory.

This weekend definitely gave the previous best Ultimate Kentucky Weekend a run for its money. So was it the best? Obviously there's a lot of factors here. The best, as I said, had to be when UK defeated LSU and Midnight Madness kicked off the Gillispie era. We were filled with hope and optimism in basketball and we had a top-10 football team.

Now we have a top-10 basketball team and our football team, which was left for dead, beat Spurrier for the first time.

Looking back, it has to be 2010 by a nose.

—Ryan

Become a Wildcat at Calipari's Basketball Experience

WHERE: Lexington

WHEN: A week in the late summer/early fall, usually September. For updated details, see www.johncaliparibasketballexperience.com.

HOW TO DO IT: There is an application process—and your wallet will be lightened severely. Only those 35 and up are eligible to play, although those 21 and up can participate as coaches.

COST FACTOR: $$\$\$\$\$\$$ ($7,495 in 2015, or $10,495 for the Captain's Club upgrade)

DIFFICULTY FACTOR: ▮ See cost factor above

BUCKET RANK: 🗑 🗑 🗑 (Five buckets for the event, one bucket for the cost, so the average is three)

HINTS FOR LITTLE WILDCATS/RELUCTANT WILDCATS:
This is an incredibly family-friendly event. Think your kids want to see the UK locker room? It's cool. Would your wife like to attend a dinner party with Coach Cal and a host of basketball celebrities at Cal's house? You're in.

His team is down three in Rupp Arena, fighting for a championship in the closing minute. The ball swings around the perimeter and he catches it. Faces up. Remembers what

Karl-Anthony Towns told him at halftime—to extend his shooting hand and follow through on the shot. Fires it. Bang! The game is tied. The crowd is raucous. Towns is pumped up. A few moments later, Coach Cal will weigh in—"That was a big shot, Shannon!"

LIFE IN THE HURRICANE

One of the questions I am periodically asked is, "What is Coach Cal really like?" I don't pretend to have a particularly meaningful answer, and this story is as close as I can come to some type of coherent response.

At the 2013 alumni game, due to an accident of position, I found myself briefly standing in a walkway at Rupp Arena with Coach Cal. Just us. He was wearing jeans and a button-down shirt, and looked like any other middle-aged guy just enjoying a casual evening. I trailed him up the walkway, at which point he came into the view of the crowd—both from the baseline seats nearest him and up above and over the lid of the walkway.

All at once, it was like a hurricane hit. From every corner, another voice shouted, "Hey coach, look up here!" "Coach, sign this." "Coach, what about (something unintelligible)." Cell phones popped out; flashes went off; basketballs materialized with Sharpies; a small swarm of people approached, and I was literally dizzy.

And the reality hit me...this is his life. He's never "off." He never really takes a vacation, or leaves his job at the office. He's always Coach Cal, and it's intense, 100% of the time. Most people reading this have probably already internalized this fact. But until you've stood in the midst of the storm, even for a few seconds, you can't really imagine what it's like.

—Joe

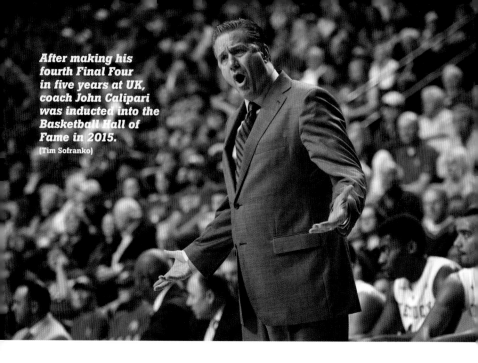

For a few moments, Shannon Ragland might forget that he's a forty-something jury verdict newsletter publisher and not a McDonald's All-American leading the Wildcats to victory. Ragland is a camper at the John Calipari Basketball Experience. "For three days," he says, "you *are* a UK player."

Indeed, for a hefty price tag, middle-aged (and sometimes older) men and women gather together to see how basketball's elite really live. They practice, put in offense and defense with successful pro and college coaches, watch game film, and play games. At the end of the camp, a lucky few are chosen for an All-Star game against a team of UK legends.

Ragland has fond memories of the all-star game. A two-year letterman at Eastern High, Ragland still has the basketball itch. And despite a vertical jump that would shame Sam Malone, he can still play. In 2013, he scored 17 points in the all-star game on 7-of-11 shooting. While the UK stars beat Ragland's team 76–41, he was the high scorer in a game against the likes of Kenny Walker, Randolph Morris, Andre Riddick, and Jared Prickett, among others.

Beyond the basketball, the camp draws repeat customers because of the interaction and experience. "Cal does everything first class," says Ragland, ticking off a list of things he appreciated—locker room, equipment, food, trainers, interaction with coaches, stats, film. Ragland played for NBA coach Del Harris in his first camp run and was chosen by college coach Dino Gaudio in his second trip. He recalled a game against Seth Greenberg's team in the camp semi-finals. "[Greenberg] puts in a little half-court trap. We turn it over twice. Dino calls time out. [He] draws up how to beat it and the problem is instantly solved."

Indeed, for those who love UK hoops but aren't physically able to participate in multiple games per day, the Experience also offers an Adolph Rupp Coach's Experience, in which the participant joins in the camp, but rather than play in the games, spends time with coaches in game preparation and management, film review, and player evaluation.

Furthermore, the Experience extends off the court. With celebrity players like the NFL's Jason Taylor and MLB's Austin Kearns and visitors like Dick Vitale and Jay Bilas, the socializing is half the fun. Add in a dinner at Cal's house in Lexington, the chance to visit with current and former UK players, and the whole event is a Big Blue dream—even if your jump shot is a bit rusty or your Xs and Os won't get you to the Final Four anytime soon.

Ragland calls the decision to attend the camp "the biggest no-brainer in the history of earth." Speaking of Calipari's family-centric vision of UK hoops, he notes, "If you come to this camp, you're in the family." Ragland notes that occasionally throughout the year, he gets an invitation to play pickup games at the Craft Center or Rupp Arena, or perhaps watch a practice or team shootaround.

It's the kind of access on which you simply cannot place a price tag. Even if you know everything about UK basketball, you probably don't know everything from the inside of UK basketball—unless you've attended the John Calipari Basketball Experience.

Go to Coach Cal's Women's Clinic (or Send Your Wife, Girlfriend, Daughter, Mom, etc.)

WHERE: Joe Craft Center and Memorial Coliseum on UK's campus

WHEN: A Saturday in September or October—follow www.coachcal.com for updates; the event lasts around three hours.

HOW TO DO IT: There is a registration process, a $100 cost, and women from 7th grade to college age are ineligible to attend (it's an NCAA issue).

COST FACTOR: $$$ There's a $100 fee, includes lunch and a free t-shirt

DIFFICULTY FACTOR: ■ Depending on gender, it's either pretty easy or impossible

BUCKET RANK: 🗑 🗑 🗑 🗑

HINTS FOR LITTLE WILDCATS/RELUCTANT WILDCATS: Much of the event is premised around semireluctant Wildcats. Just be prepared for the fact that a lot of women who very casually follow basketball come back telling spouses/kids/dads about the intricacies of the dribble-drive offense.

Whatever he did or didn't do in his UK career, Dakari Johnson was Linda Sinclair's guy. Why? Well, to know the answer, you have to have attended John Calipari's annual women's clinic. Sinclair is a retired IT specialist from Louisville. She's a lifelong Kentuckian and stands 5'1". Johnson, of course, hails from New York, stands 7'0" tall, and was one of Calipari's multitude of McDonald's All-Americans. But as the group picture of campers was organized, Johnson and Sinclair found themselves standing together. "I grabbed his hand, and he stood next to me the whole time!" Sinclair wrote of the experience. She described Johnson as "wonderful, so sweet and kind, [with] the best smile." "I am old enough to be his great-grandmother," she joked, "and he made this old lady's day."

There is no guarantee that you'll get to hold your favorite Wildcat's hand at the women's clinic. But it's not as unlikely as it might seem. "The most fun part of the camp is meeting the players," Sinclair admits. "You get to see the twinkle in their eyes and the smile that seems to be a prerequisite for any UK basketball player." Players model uniforms, chat with fans, sign autographs, and pose for pictures. Assistant coaches diagram strategies and demonstrate practice techniques.

While the man who conducts the camp has to take something of a backseat to the players, as with any event that John Calipari hosts, he makes sure to put in a thoughtful appearance. He'll run demonstration drills, field questions, and generally try to make everyone's day at the clinic a pleasant one.

The event has a very high basketball quotient. Sinclair didn't consider herself to be a basketball strategist, but after attending two of Calipari's clinics, she has some legitimate insight into the dribble-drive offense. Sessions with Rock Oliver and the UK strength coaches demonstrate the training that goes into sculpting the best Wildcats possible. In the 2014 camp, a camper ran a sprint within ten seconds of Karl-Anthony Towns' time, earning Towns a 1,000-push-up "bonus" on his next workout. Ouch! Despite the punishment which may result, the Cats put on a brave face. "You do realize that these young men are just kids," says Sinclair. "They could be your kids; they could be your neighbors. None of them come to the camp in a bad mood. They are the greatest."

Players aren't the only ones who might have to pay a physical price during the day. Campers are not exempt from to a little work, and may find themselves dribbling through cones or running through a layup line.

BERNADETTE LOCKE-MATTOX

Who: The only female assistant coach in UK men's hoops history

Why: She was a game-changer, forever demonstrating that Xs and Os matter much more on the sideline than X-and-Y chromosomes

Where to Find Her: After a decade in the WNBA, as of most recent information, Mattox was living in Lexington with her family

When Rick Pitino arrived in Lexington to take over the Kentucky coaching job, he searched for any advantage he could find. A year into his tenure, Pitino had a vacancy to fill on his staff. He thought outside the box, and told Assistant Coach Tubby Smith to dial the Georgia basketball office. The Georgia women's basketball office.

Enter Bernadette Locke, soon to be Bernadette Locke-Mattox, who had been a star player at Georgia, and then an assistant for the Georgia women's team for seven years. She added her skills and experience to a staff including Smith, Herb Sendek, and Billy Donovan,

Hoops aside, though, it is the social aspect of the event that brings the clinic attendees back again and again. The autograph session is always a high-ranking highlight, and a few lucky ladies win impressive door prizes. The coaches are not above a little gentle ribbing, but all in all, the women's clinic seems to be one event that delivers as dependably as UK basketball itself. When asked if she would recommend the camp, Sinclair pulls no punches. "Heck yes," she says. "Where else can you do this?"

and coached Wildcats like John Pelphrey, Jamal Mashburn, and Travis Ford.

"I was fortunate to be there at a time when we had good people," Locke-Mattox told the *Knoxville News-Sentinel*. She was an assistant under Pitino for four seasons, and was part of a Final Four trip, as well as perhaps the greatest game ever played, 1992's Regional Final matchup of UK and Duke.

Locke-Mattox left coaching to have a child with her husband, Vince. A year later, she was back at UK, this time as the head coach of the women's basketball program. She held the position for eight seasons, highlighted by the 1999 season, when her Cats reached the second round of the NCAA Tournament. Later, Locke-Mattox was an assistant coach with the WNBA's Connecticut Sun.

Despite her remarkable career, she is still perhaps best remembered as the first lady in the men's game at UK. "I can't say enough about how much I appreciate Rick taking a risk and C.M. [Newton, then UK athletic director] agreeing with it," Locke-Mattox told the *Knoxville News-Sentinel* in 2013. To her colleagues, she was just another coach. But to history, she was a trailblazer.

Play Pickup Basketball in Alumni Gym

WHERE: University of Kentucky campus, corner of Euclid and Limestone, Lexington, Kentucky

WHEN: There aren't a lot of times when just anyone can do this. If you're a friend of a student, or possibly someone who works there, you're good to go. Spring and winter break is a good time, as is the summer.

HOW TO DO IT: Join a club team or make a special request. Play intramurals at UK. That's a good tip.

COST FACTOR: $0. This is about who you know.

DIFFICULTY FACTOR: ▌ Difficult to do. If you're a student, it's easier.

BUCKET RANK: 🗑 Not high on the list. But if you can...definitely do it and take a pic.

HINTS FOR LITTLE WILDCATS/RELUCTANT WILDCATS:
You may not want to think too much about the little ones here. Be selfish. See if you can do this one for yourself.

. . . .

It's a little bit crazy to think that on a campus and in a gym with so much history you could sign up and play on a legendary basketball court.

But it's true.

If you're on an intramural team, or possibly on the dodgeball club squad, you've got a shot at playing in Alumni Gym. Located on the corner of Euclid and Limestone, the gym contains two basketball courts, and also houses the UK Wellness Department Body Shop. When it opened in 1924, Alumni Gym replaced Alumni Hall, which is now known as Barker Hall and Buell Armory. The 2,800-seat, $100,000 Alumni Gym was the home for the basketball squad, but now serves as a student recreation center, frequently used for intramural basketball. It's also home to the UK club dodgeball, volleyball, and basketball squads.

Yes, it is possible that guys and gals are playing dodgeball on the same court where these events occurred:

December 13, 1924: The Wildcats defeat Cincinnati in their first game in the new Alumni Gymnasium.

February 17, 1934: Fans nearly riot trying to find seats to watch UK set a new national record with its 23rd consecutive win 47–27 over Vanderbilt.

February 14, 1938: The Wildcats defeat Marquette 35–33 on Joe Hagan's 48-foot shot with seconds remaining. Gov. "Happy" Chandler marks the spot where the shot was taken by pounding a nail into the floor.

On the whole, Kentucky won 249 games in the gym, while only losing 24. Perhaps even more amazingly, UK won their last 84 games in Alumni Gym.

And it sounds like there was no home-court advantage like Kentucky's.

"Kentucky fans flocked to Alumni Gym to watch Rupp, brown suit and all, and their blue-and-white-clad heroes perform their on-court magic game after game and season after season," write Bert and Steve Nelli in *The Winning Tradition: A History of Wildcat Basketball.*

"At a typical game the building was jammed to overflowing and many fans had to be turned away. The student body is so large that there are only about 1,000 seats available to the other supporters. From the first season of Adolph Rupp's reign, Alumni Gym was generally filled to overflowing. The Kentucky–Washington & Lee game played on February 6, 1931, drew more than 4,000 of the faithful, while a contest with Georgia Tech three days later reportedly attracted nearly 5,000 Big Blue enthusiasts. One player from this era recalled in an interview 'many games in Alumni Gym where (no one) sat down from the time they came into the building until they left.'

"Opponents quickly came to dread the zealous Wildcat fans, the innovative and acid-tongued Adolph Rupp, and the multi-talented UK players," the Nellis reported. "....(They) struck fear in the hearts of opposition coaches and forced many to change their strategy."

It's a wonder if the UK club basketball team enjoys that kind of advantage. But hey—you can find out.

According to the UK website, registered UK organizations can reserve the basketball gym for approved special events once a semester. The courts are open limited hours for recreational use by UK students, faculty, and staff. Users must present a current UK student Wildcard, or current Faculty/Staff ID along with a photo ID. Alumni Gym's phone number is 859-257-1426. For reservations call 859-257-3928. Information is available online at https://www.uky.edu/campusrec/facilities/facility-reservations.

Visit Kennedy's Wildcat Den

WHERE: 405 South Limestone Street, Lexington, Kentucky. Local: 859-252-0331. Online at: Kennedys.com

WHEN: 8:30 AM–7:00 PM Monday–Thursday; 8:30 AM–5:30 PM Fridays and Saturday; noon–5 PM Sundays

HOW TO DO IT: With cash or plastic. You'll see.

COST FACTOR: $$$ It's possible to come into the store and spend a lot of money.

DIFFICULTY FACTOR: ▮ Every kind of apparel, book, and video you want is here. And if you're a student, the place is a good alternative to the campus bookstore for books and supplies.

BUCKET RANK: 🗑 🗑 🗑 Check it out. There may be some stuff in here (watches, autographed items, every kind of shirt and hat, etc.) that you may not be able to find anywhere else.

HINTS FOR LITTLE WILDCATS/RELUCTANT WILDCATS: Not a very big shop, which normally would mean you couldn't be spending a lot of time here, but UK fans will feel otherwise. Little ones may get antsy.

W hen I was a kid, it was always a treat to go visit Lexington for anything—shopping, games, dinner. I just loved it. But one of the big reasons was because I could go to stores with a lot of UK apparel, and most of it was stuff I'd never seen before.

There were always cool T-shirts, hats, and other memorabilia that was new to me (even if we would eventually get the stuff in Louisville stores a few weeks later).

One of those stores I always looked forward to was Kennedy's Wildcat Den on Limestone Street. I'd never seen such a collection of Wildcat loot.

"Privately owned and operated, Kennedy's has served the University of Kentucky community for over 60 years," the website says. "We maintain the area's largest supply of used textbooks to help students save money and buy back books every business day. Kennedy's carries textbooks for law, allied health, and independent study disciplines as well as Bluegrass Community and Technical College textbooks. Our general book section includes study aids, test preparation guides and technical handbooks."

More than that, Kennedy's has a separate facility dedicated to art, engineering, architecture, and interior design supplies. "Our Greek Shop has a wide variety of sorority and fraternity apparel and novelties," the site says.

Since 1950 the shop has been serving the community, and even today, on Kentucky Sports Radio, on the coaches' call-in shows and on the pre- and postgame radio shows, you will hear advertisements for Kennedy's. Sometimes athletes will even organize signings there.

When I was accepted into the PhD program in Educational Policy and Evaluation, my wife got me a watch from Kennedy's as a gift.

And I remember my great aunt going into stores like this and spending hundreds of dollars on holiday gifts for the family.

We think you should do that, too. You're welcome, Kennedy's!

—Ryan

Enjoy Wheeler's Pharmacy

WHERE: 336 Romany Road, Lexington

WHEN: Open 9:00 AM–7:00 PM Monday–Friday; 9:00 AM–5:00 PM Saturday; closed on Sunday

HOW TO DO IT: Drop in, preferably with an empty stomach.

COST FACTOR: $ Needless to say, walking through a pharmacy is free. Even if you need a Western omelet or a chuckwagon, it's tough to spend too much money here.

DIFFICULTY FACTOR:

BUCKET RANK:

HINTS FOR LITTLE WILDCATS/RELUCTANT WILDCATS: There is good eating here, albeit out of the 1950s–60s Americana tradition. Otherwise, unless you have some medical need or you're here to talk about the Cats, there's not much here to do.

When I was a little boy, my next-door neighbor used to babysit me while my parents worked. Her husband, Eugene, an older man who spent most of his waking hours in a recliner watching sports and TV game shows, would rise every weekday morning, shower and shave, and head to the nearby town of Neon. I wondered where he went and was told that he had gone to the local pharmacy. On one occasion, I somehow had my own business in town that necessitated that I join Eugene. His business at the local pharmacy, I discovered, was a combination of enjoying a hearty and preferably fried breakfast and righting all of the wrongs with the world, probably starting and ending with the Kentucky Wildcats.

Over the years, I've realized that in a thousand small towns in Kentucky, there are thousands of men like Eugene, eating breakfast at thousands of local pharmacies. But perhaps the foremost of these centers of Western culture has to be Wheeler's, on Romany Road in Lexington. In 1956, Buddy Wheeler graduated from UK, and two years later, he opened up the pharmacy, which became a Lexington fixture.

If talk in my corner of rural southeastern Kentucky always centered on the Wildcats, it's not hard to imagine that it did so a few miles from campus, at Wheeler's. And in fact, Wheeler's became a kind of destination, not just for those who liked to contemplate UK conversationally, but for those who actually ruled the program.

An interesting pattern has emerged over time. Coach Rupp was known for dropping in. Coach Joe B. Hall has become a constant at Wheeler's since retiring, and apparently was a regular visitor during his coaching days. Eddie Sutton couldn't find time in his busy schedule to break bread with the hardcore crowd of Wheeler's fanatics…and we all know how his coaching tenure at UK ended. Rick Pitino found his way in, as did Tubby Smith. Billy Gillispie was otherwise occupied—likely in running UK's program into the ground—and strangely never appeared. Calipari likely noticed the trend—four coaches who visited Wheeler's each won an NCAA title at UK, versus two coaches who did not visit and also didn't win, and did not last. He took no chances, coming by early and often. Notably, even after the 2012 title, Cal dropped by during ESPN's *All-Access* show to diagram strategy with ketchup-and-mustard substitutes for post players with Coach Hall, and to entertain the rest of the UK crowd with his thoughts on his team.

Make no mistake—Wheeler's is a place where celebrity sightings are not unusual, but it's not really a place to see and be seen. It's a place to pull a stool up to the counter and grab an order of French toast ($3.55); pancakes ($3.65); or the jumbo starter of two eggs, hash browns, a breakfast meat, and toast or biscuits ($8.90). The breakfast is epic, but that should not exclude their lunch and dinner menu, with choices like a deluxe hamburger ($4.15) or a fish sandwich ($4.75) with a big order of onion rings ($2.85). Save room for an authentic milkshake!

Even if no NCAA title-winning coaches are on hand, the diners at Wheeler's never lack for conversation. These folks know their basketball, and aren't shy about sharing it. The best possible compliment for Wheeler's? When I first saw the place, I felt like I was back in Neon thirty years before. Eugene has long ago passed away, but he would be at home and among friends here. As will you.

—Joe

Grab a Meal at Joe Bologna's Restaurant

WHERE: 120 West Maxwell Street, Lexington

WHEN: Open seven days a week, from 11:00 AM until at least 9:00 PM (later on weekends); call first to check at 859-252-4933.

HOW TO DO IT: Freely open to the public, does tend to get crowded on gamedays and weekends and parking can be an issue, but easy to overcome with patience and a careful eye for a spot.

COST FACTOR: $–$$

DIFFICULTY FACTOR: ▮ Might deserve a ▮ due to traffic if it's game day or the weekend, but not a real issue

BUCKET RANK: 🗑🗑 (Although ask me after a breadstick, and I'd rank it at least 🗑🗑🗑🗑)

HINTS FOR LITTLE WILDCATS/RELUCTANT WILDCATS:
There's something here for everybody. The kids' menu offers a fairly wide variety and there are lighter eating and vegetarian options. Bigger kids might appreciate the free UK posters they can nab by the checkout (mostly nonrevenue sports, but still, free is free!)

If you go to Joe Bologna's restaurant, thank your lucky stars. Remember that for a few years, the Wildcats themselves couldn't drop in for a meal. Bizarre as it seems, the NCAA actually banned the restaurant from any association with the University for three years. But we're getting ahead of ourselves, and like a good meal, a good story should be enjoyed at its own pace.

The building that now houses Joe Bologna's began its life as the Maxwell Street Presbyterian Church in 1891. The building cost $7,000 and seated 400 congregants. But the Presbyterians outgrew the facility, and in 1912, sold the building to the Ohavay Zion congregation for use as a Jewish synagogue. The building was eventually expanded, with a social hall and school added. However, by the 1980s, Lexington's Jewish community was increasingly relocating out to the suburbs, and the building was offered for sale in 1986.

Enter Joe Bologna, a native of Detroit and a former Air Force mess hall cook, who in 1973 had opened an Italian restaurant in Lexington. The new location, just four blocks from Rupp Arena, intrigued him, and in 1989, the building on Maxwell Street was transformed into an Italian restaurant—one with 41 stained-glass windows. The gorgeous woodwork and high ceiling still testify to the origins of the building, and make for a unique dining spot.

Bologna was already a fixture in the Lexington dining scene by the time of the transition to the new building, and his new location only added to his popularity. Bologna eventually catered UK's training table for four years during Tubby Smith's reign as UK head coach, and has also

EXTRA POINTS

- The tiny parking lot behind the restaurant fills up early. While there are many metered spaces nearby, please note that Lexington police are fairly vigilant against those who don't pay.

- For a few years in the early 1990s, Joe Bologna's faced stiff competition from another UK-related Italian eatery, Bravo Pitino, named for co-owner/UK coach Rick Pitino. Pitino removed his name from the restaurant in 1993, four years before he removed himself to Boston.

- For the restaurant's 40th anniversary in 2013, Bologna's special was the trademark breadstick—for 40 cents.

provided food at private events for several major UK clients, such as Smith and Mitch Barnhart. Bologna told the *Lexington Herald-Leader* in 2009, "UK just sort of grows on you, being a part of it."

However, Joe may have become too much of a part of it. A casual aside from a waitress, who mentioned to a UK compliance officer that Bologna was "comping" free food for UK athletes, led to an NCAA self-reporting by the university. Joe Bologna's was disassociated from UK athletics by order of the NCAA from 2008 to 2011. "Joe's not a bad guy," UK compliance director Sandy Bell told the *Herald-Leader*, "but he knew what he was doing."

Patrons of Joe Bologna's can readily confirm that in the kitchen, Bologna and his team certainly know what they are doing. The restaurant specializes in hefty, well-topped pizzas, available in either regular or Sicilian pan crusts. Sumptuous, large portions of pasta are readily available, and an extensive sandwich menu offers some additional options.

Two distinct treats are especially noteworthy. First, Joe and his staff can—and will—deep-fry most anything. An appetizer sampler includes deep-fried banana peppers and zucchini, among more common items like mushrooms and onion rings. Secondly, the menu's noted specialty of one breadstick is a must. One breadstick doesn't sound like much. But order it—and when you receive a giant breadstick which is basically a thinly shaped loaf of bread complete with a tub of garlic butter, you'll be glad you did.

His NCAA hiatus now past, Bologna is only too glad to welcome Wildcats and Wildcats fans. Numerous televisions are always on throughout the restaurant, and if you miss a ticket to Rupp Arena, a four-block walk to Joe's will fill your stomach, if not your need for basketball. The building on Maxwell will be packed with excited congregants—it's not a house of worship, but for Big Blue fans who enjoy with satisfied smiles, it's perhaps the next best thing.

Go to the Three Ts: Tolly-Ho, the Tin Roof, and Two Keys

WHERE: Downtown Lexington

WHEN: Preferably after, or during, a home game, or—if the Cats are on the road—when they're playing then, too.

HOW TO DO IT: Have a good time, but all things in moderation. Don't do anything stupid.

COST FACTOR: $$ Not bad at all. Prices anywhere from $3 to $10 for burgers and such. Drinks cost extra.

DIFFICULTY FACTOR: ▌ The only thing holding you back is that these places will get crowded when UK is playing. And rowdy. Get there early. Get ready for a party. And if UK wins, which they often do, the party extends to the streets outside.

BUCKET RANK: 🗑 🗑 🗑 🗑 🗑 Watch your favorite team with your favorite group—the BBN.

HINTS FOR LITTLE WILDCATS/RELUCTANT WILDCATS:
Don't like crowds? Don't like noise? Don't go. And this is definitely a place for folks who want to party. Alcohol will flow, so leave the little Big Blue kiddies at home. They can come when they're 21, because chances are, these places will still be around.

Around Lexington there are fewer places more well known than what we'll call the Three T's: Tolly-Ho, the Tin Roof, and Two Keys. Whether the Cats are playing home or away, these places will be filled with vocal UK fans. And if you can't get a ticket to the big game, or if the Wildcats are on the road, these restaurants and bars are the places you will want to spend some time. So grab a seat, or a burger, or a cheese-filled tot, or a quesadilla, or a drink—and don't forget the goldfish racing. That's a big deal, too.

Tolly-Ho: 606 S. Broadway, Lexington, (859) 253-2007, www.tollyho.com.

Here you can find the Tolly Ho burger, the Mega Ho, or the Super Ho. Fun, huh? We're not sure if this is the best place to go watch a game. By our count, there used to be a television, but this place is really for the diner food. You want to come here before or after the big game—especially if (like most of the crowd) you're trying to rebound from a night of indulging in adult beverages.

EXTRA POINTS

Visit (or Try to Visit) Idle Hour Country Club

"Chances are, they won't let you on the grounds, but you can drive around the outside of the premises of the exclusive club that was the spot for UK coaches in the 1950s," says the *Herald-Leader*.

"We had a social position coaches seldom have—good friends with Governor Wetherby and all—and we lived right there near the Idle Hour Country Club. Mr. Guy Huguelet got us an honorary membership, and that's a club that some people wait years to get into," Bear Bryant, who lived right next to Idle Hour, wrote in his autobiography.

Of course, there's another major draw nearby. "These days, if you go out the front entrance onto Richmond Road and take a right, John Calipari's house is just across the street," the *Herald-Leader* reports. Might as well check that one off the bucket list, too, eh?

AND DON'T FORGET WINCHELL'S!

While we can't include every great Lexington joint, we'd be remiss not to mention Winchell's Restaurant and Bar. Called "one of the finest sports bars you'll ever encounter" by TheDailyMeal.com, the bar is loaded with televisions, craft beer served by the pitcher (including local beers like West Sixth and Country Boy), and really good pub grub. "Don't miss the wings, barbecue pork, Kentucky beer cheese, and spicy beef nachos," the website says. Visit them: 348 Southland Drive, Lexington, (859) 278-9424.

Why here? First off, the burger's got some chops. What we mean is, like UK's basketball squad, it's really good. Ranked on many Best Burger lists throughout the country, hardly anyone can beat the price. "Since 1971, this burger joint has been racking up accolades for their delicious burgers," says TheDailyMeal.com. "The original Tolly-Ho burger is simple and perfect: a four-ounce patty on a sesame seed bun, topped with special Ho sauce, ketchup, mustard, lettuce, and onions. And best of all, it only costs $2.89!"

For what it's worth, we think the cheddar tots are what you really need. Thank us later. And go and join the "I have been drunk at Tolly-Ho" Facebook group. It's got a lot of followers.

The Tin Roof: 303 S. Limestone, Lexington, (859) 317-9111, Tinroofbars.com.

Now this is the place to watch a game. For the last Kentucky appearance in the Final Four in 2015, this was the setup: Jumbotron in a fenced-in parking lot, 16 TVs inside, five TVs in the new Bud Light Beer Garden. "Arrive by noon to get a table inside," the *Herald-Leader* recommended. "2:00–3:00 PM for outside seating. Seating will be first come, first served."

"This place is a dump but that is the essence, and one of the themes of the Tin Roof," co-owner Wes Stephens told the *Kentucky Kernel* when The Tin Roof opened in 2009. The "dump" spun off from the original Tin Roof in Nashville, and there are really only a few rules: *no spitting, no fighting,* and, from the waiters and waitresses, *my name is not "HEY!"*

There's always going to be a young crowd here, with dancing, good sandwiches, traditional New York wings, drinks, and on occasion, live music. Try the turkey Reuben and the sunny quesadilla. And if you're brave, drink a Fireball.

Two Keys: 333 S. Limestone, Lexington, (859) 254-5000, Twokeystavern.com.

With more than 40 televisions, this is another great place to watch your favorite basketball team. The tavern was named by *Travel & Leisure* as one of the best bars in the country. "Partying here should be on your bucket list," they say. "Two Keys stays open till 2:30 AM, 365 days a year, serving upward of 800 people at full tilt."

"It becomes a crazy street party off our patio after basketball games, because our whole crowd rushes outside when the Wildcats win," says general manager Courtney McGuffin.

And don't forget Tuesdays, when regulars turn up for goldfish racing. "Everyone competing gets a goldfish from our giant aquarium to race down these tiny water tracks," explains McGuffin. "The winner goes home with concert tickets or some similar prize."

That sounds like a fun party. We're in.

Chapter 3

(The Rest of) My Old Kentucky Home

You might be feeling pretty good. But even if you've watched basketball and football, had an officially sanctioned Wildcat-worthy meal, camped out in line for Big Blue Madness tickets, and hung out with Coach Cal, there's still plenty to do. Some of the folks in Lexington get mad when we remind them, but there's much more to Kentucky than what you've read so far. So get ready to hit the rest of the state. We're going through Louisville, driving down the Bourbon Trail, grabbing some barbecue, and catching up with some legendary UK characters. Let's do this!

Catch the Bluegrass Rivalry: Kentucky vs. Louisville

WHERE: Usually Lexington or Louisville, although on a couple of occasions the NCAA has provided a neutral site in the NCAA Tournament.

WHEN: The regular season game is usually right after Christmas. Any other meeting, by definition, would be in March or April.

HOW TO DO IT: Connections and money—lots of both

COST FACTOR: Solidly $$$ per person, maybe closer to $$$$ if you want a prime seat

DIFFICULTY FACTOR: ▮ Tough ticket. *Always.*

BUCKET RANK: 🗑 🗑 🗑 🗑

HINTS FOR LITTLE WILDCATS/RELUCTANT WILDCATS: To be candid, stay somewhere else. This isn't one for the half-hearted or the timid. Check out some shopping. Or visit Mary Todd Lincoln House (Lexington) or Thomas Edison house (Louisville).

• •

There are people who assert that the greatest rivalry in college basketball is between two schools in North Carolina. There were also people who asserted that the Earth was flat. They were wrong, and so are their hoops-challenged brethren. The greatest rivalry in college basketball is Kentucky and Louisville.

At the time of writing, one or the other of Kentucky's top teams has been in a participant in the last five Final Fours—including 2012, when they met in the Final Four. In 2012 and 2013, the Cats and Cardinals won back-to-back titles. The Wildcats and Cardinals have combined to win 11 NCAA Tournament titles—more than the Blue Devils and Tar Heels.

But this is the best rivalry in college basketball for reasons that have nothing to do with statistics. Carolina and Duke have always seemed like two pages out of the same ACC chapter book—bland, holier-than-thou basketball beloved by East Coast transplants who really couldn't be more similar. Carolina and Duke are like brothers who don't like each other. Kentucky and Louisville is a blood feud between two warring cultures. BBN vs. L1C4. Pitino's former Camelot vs. Pitino's...well, current employer.

Coach K has said he doesn't want to see Duke and UNC meet in the NCAA Tournament, because the loss would be too devastating for the losing fans. Kentucky and Louisville fans look forward to seeing each other in the bracket, because the results—whether U of L's Elite Eight win in 1983 or UK's Final Four victory in 2012—are that much more significant. Duke's coach hopes not to play UNC. When Kentucky plays Louisville in March, old men get into fights at dialysis clinics (really, it happened in 2012).

While Duke and UNC are guaranteed to play each other twice per year (and have since 1920), Kentucky and Louisville did not play a regular season game from 1922 to 1983. Frankly, Louisville did not arrive as a national power until Denny Crum was hired in 1971. UK and U of L nearly met in the NCAA championship game in 1975, but it was not until Crum won Louisville's first NCAA title in 1980 that the game simply *had* to happen.

After an assist from the NCAA with a regional final meeting in Knoxville in 1983, Kentucky agreed to explore an annual series. Beginning with both teams' season opener in 1983-84, the two schools have played each other annually since. In addition, a trio

RALPH BEARD: THE LEGEND FROM LOUISVILLE

Who: Faster than a locomotive, deadly on offense, and a defensive nightmare, Beard was the best point guard of his generation...if not all generations.

Why: What does it say about the UK/U of L rivalry that the player who might have had more to do with setting up the UK dynasty than any other was a Louisvillian?

Where to Find Him: Beard passed away in 2007. Find somebody who remembers him. They'll tell you how it was.

My granddad's favorite player of all time was Ralph Beard, the quicker-than-quick point guard who came to UK as a four-sport superstar athlete out of Louisville Male High School. Here's a story I wrote about meeting your favorite UK player. Originally this ran in part on the Kentucky Sports Radio website:

> Back in early 2007 I was a newspaper reporter and I was lucky enough to land a gig writing a book about UK basketball—Game of My Life: Kentucky Wildcats—where I was able to choose 30 former players and have them talk about their favorite games while at UK. (Gregg Doyel, now a columnist for The Indianapolis Star, was actually supposed to write it, but decided he couldn't and instead helped me along with it. Great dude.)
>
> It was a blast. I had the most fun I've ever had talking to these folks. But one of the best things about it was being able to meet and interview Ralph Beard, who lived in Louisville and just happened to be my Granddad's hero. Granddad said Ralph was so fast and so good with the ball he would have no problem playing in today's game.
>
> After talking with Beard and his wife, I asked if maybe I could bring my granddad by to meet him. Beard of course said yes (they just lived across town in Louisville).

My biggest thrill was taking my granddad over to meet his hero. We spent about two hours going through the Beards' basement, which was a museum of memorabilia and articles. It was just amazing. We took some pictures with them, including one of them pointing to Beard's framed gold medal from 1948.

It was a pleasure, and Beard shared his story with us, which was both heartbreaking and mesmerizing. Beard led Kentucky to an NIT and two NCAA titles—and also helped the U.S. to the gold medal in the 1948 Olympics—before graduating and playing professionally. Unfortunately, he later admitted to taking $700 from gamblers, but always denied fixing any basketball games. As punishment, he was banned for life from professional basketball. Many still say he would've been one of the game's all-time great players had he gotten to play. Instead, he went on to become a successful businessman, husband, and father.

When we left we all felt like friends, and I was proud to say I could do something for my granddad—a person who had done so much for me.

Just a few months later, in November, Ralph passed away at age 79.

But we were able to talk to him and spend time with him, and I'm so thankful for that. He was an extremely nice man, and I just wish more people knew who he was and what he meant to UK basketball.

He certainly meant a lot to me and my granddad.

Ralph Beard would be haunted by his $700 mistake for the rest of his life. But in the 1980s the tide began to turn. Beard was recognized, along with Darrell Griffith, as the best players to ever come out of Louisville. He was voted into the Kentucky Sports Hall of Fame. He was honored by his university, as well as by Louisville and Indiana (which would invite him to games as well). Former IU Coach Bob Knight brought Beard into the Hoosier locker room and introduced the former Wildcat as the "Michael Jordan of his day."

While Beard was severely punished for his action, I hope he knew how much he always meant to the fans—especially UK fans in Louisville.

Fans like my granddad.

—Ryan

of subsequent NCAA Tourney meetings have occurred. Kentucky leads the all-time series 33–15, but has had to endure its own disappointments. In 1997–98, Tubby Smith's first team lost to the Cardinals, but went on to win the NCAA championship hardware. Louisville fans taunted with "first in the nation, second in the state" T-shirts. With Kentucky winning seven of John Calipari's first eight meetings in the series, many in the Wildcat camp wonder if Pitino's fifteen seconds—oops, minutes—of fame are up.

At the end of the day, fans of each school have rooted for the other during NCAA title runs, but when the Cats and Cardinals meet, there is no question of divided loyalty. Rivalry burns red hot in Lexington and Louisville. Watching the two schools play might not be fun for your garden-variety casual follower, but for the hardcore fan, the stakes are unequaled when the Cats play the Cardinals—especially in Louisville's home, the Yum! Center, on the banks of the Ohio in the downtown part of the city.

Most UK fans will have to admit that the Yum! Center may be the finest basketball venue in America. Amazing sightlines, up-to-the-minute technology and a cozy feel give the Cards a real home-court advantage for fans. But even so, Kentucky fans still get in when (every other season) UK visits the Yum! Center to play Louisville.

In fact, UK fans get in so often, and create such havoc, the Cards' athletic director Tom Jurich and their basketball coach Rick Pitino have complained to their own fans to not sell tickets to those rooting for UK. It doesn't matter. The Blue Mist gets in. And when they do, it may just be the best environment in all of college basketball. A UK–U of L game in Rupp Arena is great. But when the game is in Louisville it's truly special. And it's something you have to see. Then again, a Calipari team has only lost once to Louisville—a three-point defeat in the Yum! Center in December 2012. So it may not matter to the teams at all where they play. UK seems to dominate in Lexington, in Louisville, and on neutral courts in the NCAA Tournament. Get to one of those games if you can.

See Cat City West: Louisville!?

If you're looking for true-blue Wildcat backers, sites, and events, one of the last places you'd look should be one of the first—Louisville. In the belly of the beast, as it were, lies a huge collection of fun UK-related landmarks and events. Here are a few of the highlights:

Louisville Gardens: In downtown Louisville, at what is now Sixth Street and Muhammad Ali Boulevard, was the city's first great basketball palace. While it was home to the Louisville Cardinals beginning in 1945, the building also hosted the SEC Tournament from 1941 to 1952, when the SEC cancelled the event for a few decades. The Wildcats also played a game or two per year there otherwise, and ended up posting a 61–11 mark in the building between 1937 and 1956.

The Gardens was built in 1905, and while it sits in disrepair today, it also hosted events as significant and diverse as concerts from Louis Armstrong and Elvis Presley to speeches from Harry Truman and Dr. Martin Luther King Jr. While today it is essentially vacant, it is a prominent UK site, and is within walking distance of the Muhammad Ali Center, the Kentucky Performing Arts Center, the Louisville Slugger museum, and a variety of tasty restaurants.

Freedom Hall: In 1956, the Louisville Cardinals moved to Freedom Hall. Two years later, UK took over, winning the NCAA Championship in the facility. Aside from Kentucky–Louisville games, the Cats played an annual game at Freedom Hall until 2012. They posted a 60–18 mark in the arena, including many wins over Indiana

WINSTON BENNETT

Who: A hard-working, intense power forward who is still 22nd on the career UK scoring list

Why: Because Bennett indicated a changing of the order in inner-city Louisville recruiting, and played a big part in slaying the ghosts of Kentucky's past.

Where to Find Him: Bennett lives in western Kentucky. He sells insurance and speaks to young people these days. His book, *Fight for Your Life*, also shares his story

Before Winston Bennett, the city of Louisville was colored anything but blue—mostly Louisville Cardinal red or Western Kentucky red. Even after Bennett's college career, in the 1990s, Rick Pitino told author Eddie Einhorn that he was unprepared for the hatred of African American Louisvillians toward Kentucky when he (unsuccessfully) recruited Dwayne Morton. These days, for the most part, that legacy of negativity is mostly a distant memory—but the situation changed mostly with the recruitment of Winston Bennett.

and Notre Dame, opponents for whom Freedom Hall served as a neutral site.

Another fun aspect of Freedom Hall is that members of the Kentucky Athletic Hall of Fame, many of whom were Wildcats, are honored with brass plaques that line the corridor of the arena. While Freedom Hall is not regularly used now, it is very accessible during the annual state fair. And who can't use a good excuse to eat deep-fried snacks and marvel at gigantic vegetables?

Bennett was an all-everything power forward at Louisville Male High School. Denny Crum recalled in 2013 that Bennett had been a Louisville Cardinal ball boy and had played in Crum's summer camps. Conventional wisdom was that he would become the next of many African American Male High stars to play at U of L. But conventional wisdom was wrong.

"I grew up in a time where there was a racial cloud over the Kentucky program in terms of how African Americans in Louisville felt about UK," Bennett admitted in 2013. "But my parents had always taught me to go and see things for yourself."

Bennett went, saw things for himself, and became a Wildcat. He scored 1,399 points as a Wildcat and played in the Final Four as a freshman. After a brief NBA career, Bennett became a coach and was part of Rick Pitino's staff for the 1996 NCAA title team.

The Louisville-to-UK connection would be further utilized over the years, perhaps most notably with Derek Anderson, Scott Padgett, and Rajon Rondo. But it was Winston Bennett who opened the pipeline and forever changed UK's image for the better.

The YUM! Center: As a frequent NCAA site, the YUM! Center is a hot property for Cat fans who can't score home tickets. UK's 6–1 record in the building doesn't hurt.

Wildcat Hometown: Much to the dismay of Cardinal backers, a great number of legendary Wildcats grew up in Louisville. Louisville's high school circuit is like a UK history lesson, from Doss (Derek Anderson) to Male (Ralph Beard, Winston Bennett) to Eastern (Rajon Rondo, before he transferred to Oak Hill Academy) to St. X (Scott Padgett). Given the local connections of Wildcat legends, it's never hard to find a local who can tell you stories of high school glory for the local kids who went on to wear blue.

The Tin Roof: If you can't score UK/U of L tickets, the Tin Roof seems to be the de facto UK headquarters in Louisville. Located at 3921 Shelbyville Road (and thus close to the city's main mall thoroughfares), if a Cat fan needs a good environment to have a burger and a beverage, it's always a good call.

EXTRA POINTS

Wildcat Honor Roll: Big Blue Highlights from the Rivalry

A top five of unforgettable UK/U of L moments:

1. The 2012 Final Four win. Anthony Davis had 18 points, 14 rebounds, and five blocked shots in a 69–61 win in the national semifinal. UK won title No. 8 two nights later, but it wasn't any sweeter than this win.

2. The 2014 NCAA Tournament win. Kentucky came from behind to win in the Sweet Sixteen 74–69. Aaron Harrison continued his run of late-season theatrics, with a big three to give UK the lead in the final minute.

3. In December 2001, new Louisville coach Rick Pitino experienced his return to Rupp. Kentucky won the game 82–62, while Cat fans serenaded his successor with chants of "TU-BBY TU-BBY!"

4. In December 1986, the defending NCAA champion Cardinals were crushed 85–51, with UK favorite and native Kentuckian Rex Chapman nearly bringing down the roof with 26 points, including a couple of mammoth dunks.

5. In December 1987, with UK down by one in the closing seconds, and everyone in Rupp Arena expecting Chapman to take the last shot, senior Cedric Jenkins tipped in Ed Davendar's miss just ahead of the buzzer to win the game 76–75.

Derby Festival Basketball Clinic: Every spring an exhibition game of high school all-stars takes place in Freedom Hall. The game's organizers make an effort to involve future Cardinals and Wildcats, although a large number of Cats these days are bound for more prestigious all-star games. That said, the chance to see future Cats and Cards, as well as a variety of other top-flight players from around the country, is a rare treat. The game's alumni list includes Moses Malone, Isiah Thomas, Dominique Wilkins, Doc Rivers, Penny Hardaway, and Zack Randolph, in addition to a ton of Wildcat stars (Sam Bowie, Rex Chapman, Jamal Mashburn, Scott Padgett, Bobby Perry, etc.).

The Kentucky Derby: While the event has no direct relation to UK, there is no Kentucky event offering the capacity to see and be seen quite like the annual Kentucky Derby. Beginning in 1875, some of the fastest thoroughbred horses in the world faced off at Churchill Downs in Louisville for a race that has gradually become equal parts sports event and spectacle. As for the Kentucky quotient, the prestigious Barnstable Brown gala often features several prominent Wildcats on its much-hyped guest list. In 2014, the list included Jodie Meeks, Doron Lamb, Darius Miller, and football star Randall Cobb, along with a multitude of actors, musicians, and people famous for being famous. If you blink, you might miss the most important part of the race, but the party lasts for days.

Bear in mind that in Louisville, while the fans, players, and even (somehow) coaches are mostly civil, it's sometimes barely civil. In March 2014, before the UK–U of L Sweet 16 matchup, Louisville mayor Greg Fischer proclaimed a "Cardinal Red Day," asking fans to wear red to support the Cardinals. I was on business in Louisville that day and got out of my car to immediately see a gentleman in a white T-shirt on which he had painted—in giant blue letters—"**** you, Mayor Fischer."

—Joe

Do the Autograph Tour Thing

WHERE: Usually in shops across the state

WHEN: Immediately after the season. Usually late March to early April. This is when the players graduate and/or sign with agents.

HOW TO DO IT: Pay attention to the media and KSR for schedules, then be prepared to wait in line.

COST FACTOR: $ to $$$. Willie Cauley-Stein's autograph went for $35.

DIFFICULTY FACTOR: █ It isn't difficult if you're okay to wait in lines and pay the dough.

BUCKET RANK: 🗑 🗑 🗑 🗑 🗑 It's the best way to meet your UK heroes.

HINTS FOR LITTLE WILDCATS/RELUCTANT WILDCATS: The lines, and the wait, can be long, but if you want Junior to have his picture taken with a ball player this is the best way to do it. Grab some things to keep them occupied while you wait.

- -

I looked at my watch. I had 15 minutes.

Still basking in the glow of the Wildcats' eighth national championship, I'd gone out to a celebratory dinner with my wife, daughter, and parents. Being that my parents lived in Louisville but we lived in northern Kentucky, it was something we rarely got to do. But I had a secret agenda.

I knew that if I timed it just right I may be able to go over to the Cardboard Heroes in the Florence Mall to meet recently crowned Final Four Most Outstanding Player Anthony Davis.

You see, at the conclusion of every season, Kentucky's players have been known to organize autograph tours across the state, where UK fans can wait in line—sometimes for hours—to meet their heroes and get a picture or an autograph. It's a neat setup, and one we recommend you try.

As for me in 2012, I was cutting it close. The session ended at 7:00 PM, and I arrived at 6:50. But here's the good thing: I was last in line, and there weren't very many people in front of me. I couldn't believe it. This guy was going to be the No. 1 pick in the NBA Draft. He may even make the Olympic team.

I quickly took the last spot in line. A few minutes later, I was up in front, chatting up Anthony Davis.

I'd brought two posters for him to sign. I believe I paid $50 total for the autographs, which now looks like a bargain. The posters are framed and hanging in my guest room.

But in 2012, Davis had yet to sign a contract, win a gold medal, or be named to an all-star team. He was just a kid. I congratulated him on leading his team to the 2012 championship.

I asked him if he was ever nervous.

"Naw, man—we knew we were going to win," he told me. "We just knew. We had the best team and the best coaches and we were confident."

I nodded. I told him I felt the same way. But it didn't stop me from being nervous.

"So where do you think you're headed in the draft?" I asked.

He just pointed to the cap he was wearing. New Orleans. "No. 1, baby," he said.

Later that summer, he was right. He was the No. 1 pick in the NBA Draft—and he went to New Orleans.

There are few things in my collection of memorabilia that I truly treasure—but I'm glad I went out to meet Anthony Davis. He very well could be the most successful pro player to ever come out of Kentucky, and I was happy I got a few words with him.

Unfortunately, I had no real camera phone at the time. So the one thing I don't have is a good picture of Davis and me. Never forget to bring your camera to these things.

McFARLANE SPORTSPICKS FIGURES

Remember Starting Lineup figures? If you don't, do you remember Macaulay Culkin shooting down his sports figures with a BB gun in *Home Alone*? Those were Starting Lineups the cheap, posable sports toys by Kenner that sold like hotcakes in the late 1980s and 1990s. Several UK Wildcats were featured in sets of those toys, including Antoine Walker and Ron Mercer in their Kentucky uniforms (find them on eBay).

The current version of those toys are McFarlane SportsPicks from comic-book creator Todd McFarlane. These are taller, much more detailed versions of the action figures. And they, too, have created some former UK toys.

Here's a look at the former UK figures they've made:
- Rajon Rondo
- Tayshaun Prince
- Brandon Webb (baseball)
- John Wall
- Anthony Davis (two figures)
- Eric Bledsoe

Collect them all!

Someday I'll get a pic with him. But I may have to pay a lot more for the opportunity.

We highly recommend these kinds of signing opportunities. You never know when you may be meeting the next great pro player. In just the last few years I was able to meet the starting five players from the 2012 title team: Brandon Knight, Darius Miller, Nerlens Noel, and Rex Chapman.

I remember back in 1994, I stood in line to see Jeff Brassow at the Allied Sporting Goods in Dixie Manor in south Louisville. I cringed when the elderly, obese man wearing a UK shirt in front of me told the former player this:

"Jeff, I just wanted you to know that you played exactly like I did."

I'm just going to guess that the last time the old man played was about a thousand years ago. It probably involved an actual peach basket, and maybe Dr. Naismith too.

But Jeff just smiled and said thank you. Then I was able to get my own personal Brassow autograph.

—Ryan

The UK autograph tours will take players all across the state.

Here's an example of a few days from Dakari Johnson and Trey Lyles' autograph-tour itinerary after the 2015 season:

Friday: Elizabethtown Mall, 6:00–7:30 PM

Saturday: Hillbilly Days Appalachian Wireless Booth, Pikeville, 10:00 AM–noon

Saturday: Wildcats 'N More, Dry Ridge, 6:00–7:30 PM

Sunday: Barleycorns, Cold Spring, Noon–1:30 PM

Tuesday: Wildcats Sports Apparel, Nicholasville, 6:00–7:30 PM

Take in a KSR Tour Stop

WHERE: All over the state of Kentucky, sometimes just outside the state lines, such as in West Virginia

WHEN: Always 10:00 AM–noon, particularly in eight weeks during the summer, but you can find KSR stops in Louisville and Lexington throughout the basketball and football seasons, too.

COST FACTOR: $0. Just show up and listen—you may even win free tickets!

DIFFICULTY FACTOR: ▌ All you need to know is where they're going to be. Just show up early!

BUCKET RANK: 🗑 Seeing Matt Jones and Ryan Lemond in front of a crowd is seeing them in their element. It's definitely worth it—and you never know what giveaways or special guests (Coach Calipari, maybe? Ashley Judd?) may stop by.

HINTS FOR LITTLE WILDCATS/RELUCTANT WILDCATS: Not a whole lot to do here for little guys and gals. It's early, and there's a lot of talking. They may need to stay at home for this one.

W hat else could bring 200-plus people out for a radio station remote broadcast in the wee hours of the morning—to a mattress store, no less? Or a parking lot? Or a golf course on a stormy day?

It must be Matt Jones, Ryan Lemond, and Kentucky Sports Radio, whom you previously met in the Ultimate Game Day Experience. If you've never been to one of their "live remote" shows, you need to put it on your bucket list, so you can scratch it off.

In 2005, Jones started KentuckySportsRadio.com, and each day tens of thousands of sports fans visit the website for news about Kentucky and their rivals. On weekdays, from 10:00 AM to noon (or sometimes delayed in some markets) those fans tune in to listen to Jones, former Lexington sportscaster Lemond, and web writer Drew Franklin, as they ponder the news of the day on their radio show. Sometimes they take that show on the road, visiting one of their sponsors or piling into a local McDonald's or pizzeria.

Then, for several weeks in the summer, they pack up to visit each of their 31 affiliates. This is where the real party begins, as hundreds of fans show up to greet the stars. The best way to find out where the tour will be? Listen to the show.

"Last summer, Jones and sidekicks Ryan Lemond and Drew Franklin spent five weeks doing remote radio broadcasts all over the state," reported the *Herald-Leader*.

"When the tour came to Lexington, hundreds showed up at Whitaker Bank Ballpark to watch them talk. Nearly 200 fans attended their remote broadcast October 4 from an asphalt basketball court behind Memorial Coliseum. That was during the annual campout of UK fans waiting to get tickets for Big Blue Madness, the official start of basketball practice."

Whether to listen for news, for entertainment, or to win tickets to an event, there are number of reasons why people show up to a KSR remote. But above all else, it's about the love of the Big Blue.

The *Herald-Leader* talked to Jeff Swann, who listens to the KSR show each morning in Louisville while he works at the Ford Motor Company assembly plant. He came out to a remote appearance and got Jones' autograph.

"We get a kick out of the callers," Swann told the newspaper. "And he has good guests."

KSR Affiliate List

(Subject to change)

WCBL (1290 AM): Benton
WBGN (1340 AM): Bowling Green
WTCO (1450 AM): Campbellsville
WAIN (93.9 FM): Columbia
WHIR (1230 AM): Danville
WVHI (1330 AM): Evansville, IN (delayed)
WCLU (1490 AM): Glasgow
WGOH (1370 AM): Grayson
WHOP (95.3 FM): Hopkinsville
WJKY (1060 AM): Jamestown
WMTL (870 AM): Leitchfield (delayed)
WLAP (630 AM): Lexington
WFTG (1400 AM): London
WKJK (1080 AM): Louisville
WFMW (730 AM): Madisonville
WWXL (1450 AM): Manchester
WFTM (1240 AM): Maysville
WRIL (106.3 FM): Middlesboro (delayed)
WKYM (101.7 FM): Monticello
WMSK (1550 AM): Morganfield
WLBQ (1570 AM): Morgantown (delayed)
WLME (102.7 FM):Owensboro
WPAD (1560 AM): Paducah
WKYH (600 AM): Paintsville
WLSI (900 AM): Pikeville
WPRT (960 AM): Prestonsburg
WSFC (1240 AM): Somerset
WTCW (920 AM): Whitesburg
WHAY (98.3 FM): Whitley City
WBTH (1400 AM): Williamson

Check out the Bourbon Trail

WHERE: Across the heart of Kentucky's bluegrass region, but specific sites can vary

WHEN: During standard business hours, as noted individually below

HOW TO DO IT: Mostly, however you please. There is a cool feature on the kybourbontrail.com website, advising you of ways to bike the Trail.

COST FACTOR: $–$$ mostly. Depends on how involved in sampling the goods or purchasing souvenirs one becomes.

DIFFICULTY FACTOR: ▌All aspects aren't entirely family friendly

BUCKET RANK: 🗑 🗑 🗑 🗑

HINTS FOR LITTLE WILDCATS/RELUCTANT WILDCATS:
Assuming you're not too squeamish about the underlying idea of alcohol consumption, there generally are interesting sites and stories even for teetotalers or children.

Bluegrass, basketball, and bourbon. Even if the grass isn't really blue, and the basketball doesn't go on year round, the bourbon is always smooth and pure. If you enjoy Kentucky history—and a little bit of a unique twist on Wildcat lore—the Bourbon Trail is a fun way to see some of the state, perhaps have a drink or two, and pass the offseason days.

Arguments about particular brands, and even tour stops, could be as fierce as those over an all-time Wildcat starting five. But here are a few of the highlights, with possible Wildcat connections or features.

Maker's Mark Distillery is in tiny Loretto, Kentucky (3350 Burkes Spring Road). Your GPS may struggle to find the place, but connoisseurs of bourbon know the way. Maker's Mark is aged not by time, but by taste. When the tasters on site decide a batch is ready— usually 6 to 7½ years after it was barreled— it's ready for sale. A highlight of their tour (Monday–Saturday 9:30 AM–4:30 PM; Sun [March-December] 11:30 AM–4:30 PM; $9) is the opportunity to dip your own bottle in the distinctive red sealing wax. As for a Wildcat connection, Maker's Mark has created special collectible bottles for many UK-related themes. A denim bottle celebrated the 1996 Wildcat NCAA champs (who wore denim uniforms). A 2012 championship bottle also circulates, and a "blue-over-red" bottle was prepared in 2001, when UK beat Louisville in the annual basketball matchup. Most recently, an Adolph Rupp bottle debuted.

Jim Beam has its stillhouse in Clermont, Kentucky (526 Happy Hollow Road). The Beam family has made whiskey since 1795, and the expertise shows in its product. While the means of distribution have changed in 220 years, the smooth, well-aged product has not. A tour is a fun way to pass an hour or two (tours Monday–Saturday 9:30 AM–3:30 PM; Sun 12:30–3:30 PM; $10). Current distiller Fred Noe is a seventh generation Beam—and a UK alum and Wildcat backer. One of the brand's "small batch" bourbon collection shares a name with the original Wildcat basketball All-American, Basil Hayden, who must've been drinking something good, as he managed to be the only known Wildcat to live in three centuries (1899–2003). Unfortunately, the name appears to be a coincidence, but hey, if there was a drink called "Pat Riley's" or "Jack Givens'," would we need to split a hair?

Four Roses in Lawrenceburg is headquartered in a Spanish Mission-style building (1224 Bonds Mill Road, tours Monday–Saturday 9:00 AM–3:00 PM; Sunday noon–3:00 PM; $5). It might just cause Cat fans to remember the Alamo—and San Antonio, where Tubby Smith's

BASIL HAYDEN

Who: The first UK basketball All-American, and the oldest Wildcat in memory

Why: The man was a living great story. He lived in three centuries, he was an All-American, and he was the most unsuccessful coach in UK history.

Where to Find Him: NOT in bourbon circles—the bourbon that bears his name is actually named for a different Basil Hayden, oddly enough

UK's first All-American in basketball was 5'11" and weighed 165 pounds in his prime. He averaged just under 10 points per game during his All-American season, and scored 333 points in his UK career. But Basil Hayden was a playmaker, and he made enough plays to help UK to an SIAA championship, which was probably the school's first step in building up a huge basketball tradition.

Hayden was born in 1899, and after his playing days, he went on to coach UK for a solitary season in 1926–27, when the squad went 3–13 under his leadership. Hayden told Russell Rice in *The Wildcats,* "I couldn't get a very good effort out of them all season." Hayden went on to teach school, work for a bank, serve as a hospital administrator, and work for the Kentucky conference of the United Methodist Church.

He lived until 2003, famously declaring that the secret to longevity was to live to be 99, and then be real careful. For the man who had been drafted for World War I, it was an amazing life to live to see UK basketball, as well as himself, turn 100 years old.

1998 squad won an NCAA title. Four Roses cultivates its bourbon in single-story warehouses in order to provide more consistent aging and taste to its products. Lawrenceburg also happens to have been the home—and is the final resting place—of Mr. Wildcat, Bill Keightley. A toast to Mr. Bill is always appropriate.

Wild Turkey is also in Lawrenceburg (1417 Versailles Road, tours Monday–Saturday 9:00 AM–4:00 PM; Sunday 10:00 AM–3:00 PM). Wild Turkey obtains a signature flavor by distilling its bourbon at a lower proof than the other brands. The intended effect is to require less addition of water, and a taste closer to exactly what comes in the

Heaven Hill's Bourbon Heritage Center, located in Bardstown, Kentucky, is a great place to learn about the rich history of bourbon making as well as taste critically acclaimed bourbons. (AP Images)

warehoused barrels. As for popularity, ESPN's Mark Schlabach listed Wild Turkey as the quasi-official UK "beverage of choice" in his UK–Louisville Tale of the Tape for the 2012 Final Four matchup.

Woodford Reserve is Kentucky's oldest and smallest distillery, producing bourbon on site in Versailles (7855 McCracken Pike, tours Monday–Saturday 10:00 AM–3:00 PM; Sunday 1:00 PM–3:00 PM; $10) since 1797. One of the more interesting parts of Woodford's building is the "flavor wheel" at the end of their tour, which helps guests understand the bevy of tastes that blend and age into quality Kentucky bourbon. Given the close proximity of Woodford to Lexington, a bourbon-and-basketball doubleheader is always a possibility.

The other stops on the Bourbon Trail:

Bulleit Frontier Whiskey, 3860 Fitzgerald Road, Louisville, Kentucky (Wednesday–Sunday 10:00 AM–2:00 PM; $10);

Heaven Hill Bourbon Heritage Center, 1311 Gilkey Run Road, Bardstown, Kentucky (March–December, Monday–Saturday 10:00 AM–3:40 PM; Sun noon–2:40 PM; closed on Sunday and Monday in January and February; $10);

Town Branch Bourbon, 401 Cross Street, Lexington, Kentucky (Monday–Saturday 10:00 AM–4:00 PM, Sunday noon–4:00 PM; $8.50);

Evan Williams Bourbon, 528 West Main Street, Louisville, Kentucky (Monday–Thursday 11:00 AM–4:30 PM; Friday–Saturday 10:00 AM–5:00 PM, Sunday 1:00 PM–4:30 PM; $12).

Enjoy a UK Game at One of Kentucky's Great Local Barbecue Joints

Kentucky is traditionally known for basketball and bourbon. And while the reasoning is solid, unfortunately, most outsiders don't recognize a third "b" that is just as deserving of mention—barbecue. In the same way that ESPN will gab about the Big Ten's top school or Duke's latest feat, foodies will talk about Kansas City 'cue or Carolina pig, but don't tease yourself—they may have the good stuff, but the best stuff is in Kentucky.

What exactly is barbecue? Well, academics and foodies might debate it, but in the greater sense of the word, it's smoked meat—preferably smoked slowly in an open pit. Great debates can break out over exactly how long to smoke the meat, and which type of wood to use, etc.

Perhaps the best feature of Kentucky's barbecue culture is how multifaceted it is. In central-to-western Kentucky, mutton (that's sheep, for the outsiders) is a hidden barbecue delight—as is burgoo, something between a soup, a stew, and the best liquefied barbecue concoction imaginable. In south central Kentucky, pork shoulder is sliced ultra thin and served with a vinegar dip that will rarely fail to delight. Out near Lexington and Louisville, you might find ribs, either in the Kansas City or Memphis style, or brisket, long-smoked and well-seasoned. There is no single Kentucky barbecue any more than there is a single Kentucky identity. You can travel from Paducah to Pikeville, from Owensboro to Tompkinsville, and never taste the exact same flavor twice.

So where to start? At virtually any spot in the commonwealth of Kentucky (although unfortunately, rather rarely in the eastern end), good barbecue is readily available. Here are a few favorites, particularly noted for UK connection:

Sarah's BBQ (720 Henry Clay Boulevard, Lexington) is a fun stop. I knew I was in Cat fan central when I saw the autograph of one of my favorite Cats—Cedric Jenkins—over the air hockey table. UK paraphernalia and TVs dot the restaurant. Owners LD and Ralph Egbert aren't shy about serving up some top-flight 'cue (I loved the ribs, and my wife raved about their pulled-pork nachos)—or about their love of the Cats.

Roy's BBQ (101 Sarah Lane, Russellville) is both local for me and phenomenal. Roy's pulled-pork sandwiches and fried dill-pickle spears are worth a stop anytime, and I love their lemon pie. The restaurant's back room is thoroughly decked out in UK gear, and when I stopped by just before the most recent UK/U of L game, the cashier bemoaned having to work during the game—and then assured me, he'd be watching on the in-store TVs.

O'Tyme Hickory Pit (1535 Broad Street, Paducah) is run by some good folks who love the Cats. Drop by and scan the walls if you don't believe it. O'Tyme is locally noted for their barbecue ham. If it's meat, and you can smoke it, it's worth checking out!

Moonlite (2840 West Parrish Avenue, Owensboro) is a foodie staple. Joe B. Hall is among the multitude of celebrities who are on their autographed photo wall of fame. If he and Eddie Sutton grabbed Moonlite when they recruited Rex Chapman out of Owensboro, it's a wonder that they ever left town. That said, the finicky barbecue eaters will tell you that the sides at Moonlite are great, but the 'cue across town at **Old Hickory** (338 Washington Avenue, Owensboro) is even better. Ryan and I gathered with a friend at Old Hickory and ate the better part of a pig as research for this book. Tough work, but somebody had to do it.

There is of a multitude of legendary barbecue joints in Tompkinsville. The pork shoulder in the tiny seat of Monroe County is a must. My personal pick is **R&S** (217 South Jackson Street), although I've never gone elsewhere to see if the food is better (because I'm not sure that would be possible). I enjoyed a UK–UT basketball game there a couple of years ago. UK won, and I was very well fed.

Red State (4020 Georgetown Road) is another Lexington tradition with a delightfully UK-related flavor. Where else can you enjoy some ribs or brisket in a restaurant where Sam Bowie and Kenny "Sky" Walker have marked their heights on the wall?

If you're in need of more suggestions, I can't place a strong enough recommendation on Wes Berry's *Kentucky Barbecue Book.* In full disclosure, Wes is a professor at Western Kentucky University, but he says he supports all of the state's basketball teams. And he definitely supports a good dinner or two, and has led me unfailingly to them.

—Joe

• •

Meet Kentucky Elvis

Of course he's got blue suede shoes. But for Rick Cothern, they're probably more like Big Blue suede shoes.

Fans, you'll see this guy in full Elvis garb everywhere from his hometown of Bowling Green, Kentucky, to cheering for his beloved Big Blue Kentucky Wildcats in Lexington, to cheering for his beloved Tennessee Titans in Nashville. He's everywhere—and chances are, the television cameras aren't far behind him.

Yes, for those wondering, he is a professional Elvis impersonator. But that's not how all this began. Back in the mid-1990s, Cothern went to Titans games and he wanted to stand out, so he wore crazy masks, like those of past presidents Jimmy Carter or Ronald Reagan. It got him attention, and sometimes it got him on TV.

"When I was young I watched all these crazy characters that helped create the ambiance," Cothern told the *Bowling Green Daily News* in an interview. "I never thought I'd be one of those crazy characters."

But he is.

One year, when the SEC Tournament was held in Memphis, he came as the hometown icon Elvis Presley, and Cothern's world changed. He even brought his two stepsons to Titans games dressed like little Elvis impersonators. Suddenly, during Kentucky games he was on TV as much as Rick Pitino. Newspapers did stories. He was a pseudo-celebrity.

He was featured on *Monday Night Football*. And at the SEC Tournament. And at the Final Four.

Personally, I remember meeting him for the first time at Big Blue Madness. It was probably 10 years ago. I decided to get a picture with him—but of course I had to get in line. There were two old ladies decked out in UK gear in front of me.

At that point, the comical absurdity of waiting in line to have my picture taken with a fan dressed like Elvis dawned on me. But there was no going back. I did it anyway. No regrets, either. Cothern was the nicest guy in the world. He was in full character—took a pic with me and said, "Go Big Blue!"

—Ryan

Play Some Pickup at Rupp Arena North

WHERE: Ted Arlinghaus' place, Edgewood, Kentucky

WHEN: You should probably call ahead

COST FACTOR: No cost

DIFFICULTY FACTOR: ● If the Arlinghauses know you, you can play. Or if you're in a league in northern Kentucky, you may have a shot, too.

BUCKET RANK: 🗑 🗑 🗑 You do feel like you're playing in Rupp Arena

HINTS FOR LITTLE WILDCATS/RELUCTANT WILDCATS: The little kids can play, too!

Ted Arlinghaus has a Big Blue backyard.

Or, to put it another way, he has Big Blue in his backyard. Flash back to 1992, when Arlinghaus, a successful construction business owner in Edgewood, Kentucky, had an idea to build a basketball court for his family.

"We really just wanted to build something for the kids," says Arlinghaus, now 65. "We had 10 kids. But then we built it, and it was just an enclosed goal but it was something we really liked. Then we just kept adding more and more to it. It became a full court, then it became a full gym. Then it took on more of a UK thing."

A COLLECTION FOR THE AGES

John Carpenter, of tiny Firebrick, Kentucky, has the autographs of all the championship-winning coaches from UK, except one. Those would be, if you're keeping score at home, coaches Adolph Rupp, Joe B. Hall, Rick Pitino, "Tubby" Smith—and the last one, the one he needs—John Calipari.

You see, Carpenter, a 57-year-old Lewis County resident, has what has been called the largest private collection of sports memorabilia in the world, by *Ripley's Believe It or Not*. And yes, there are a lot of non-UK-related items in the collection. There's a bobblehead of his own likeness, given to him by none other than former New York Yankees owner George Steinbrenner. There's a Tennessee Lady Vols jersey autographed by former head coach Pat Summitt. There's a Babe Ruth baseball and a Jim Thorpe shoe.

In all, there are more than 6,000 pieces of memorabilia stacked from floor to ceiling in his modest home. Carpenter has been featured on ESPN for his collection, and he's even graced the cover of his own Wheaties box.

But he still needs Cal's signature. "I have it on a UMass picture," Carpenter says, explaining he received Calipari's autograph through the mail when Calipari was a coach at Massachusetts. "But I need it on something that says Kentucky."

A nice man from Illinois sent Carpenter Adolph Rupp's signature through the mail. Maybe another nice UK fan could do the same.

Carpenter welcomes all to his home to see the endless memorabilia. He'll even bring out some of his most prized possessions to show you. Just settle in—because you could be there for a good, long while.

At the same time, down in Lexington, UK Coach Rick Pitino had things rolling. His team was already a contender again, after just three seasons coming off probation. "We loved that team so much," Arlinghaus said.

They were, in a word, Unforgettable. John Pelphrey. Deron Feldhaus. Richie Farmer. Sean Woods. Jamal Mashburn.

So it just seemed natural for Arlinghaus to build his court to regulation size, with the same dimensions and paint as to look like Rupp Arena. In fact, he called the place "Rupp Arena North."

And that's when it started attracting attention.

Through friends of friends, Arlinghaus was able to send an art work to the UK players, which they signed. That was also incorporated into the court—a special tribute to the team the Arlinghaus family loved so much.

Throughout the years the family opened up the court to the community. You'd see the kids' neighborhood teams practicing there, along with high school teams and pickup leagues. If you knew the family, you could play. Even more than 20 years later it still serves as a rec center for the locals.

"We like to share it as much as possible," Arlinghaus says. "The folks around here love their basketball—especially UK basketball."

Want to play at Rupp Arena North? All you need to do is call ahead.

Roger Laws, of northern Kentucky, may have the largest collection of UK memorabilia in the world. But you have to get an invitation to see it. (Ryan Clark)

Visit "No. 1 Fan" Roger Laws' Barn—If You Can

WHERE: Rural Northern Kentucky

WHEN: Whenever you're invited

COST FACTOR: $ You've got to pay for the gas to get there

DIFFICULTY FACTOR: ▌ You must be invited. It's the only way.

BUCKET RANK: 🗑 🗑 🗑 🗑 If you get the invite, go! You will be amazed.

HINTS FOR LITTLE WILDCATS/RELUCTANT WILDCATS:
Lots of breakables. Leave the little ones at home.

. . . .

There are stories of amazing collections of Kentucky memorabilia. Then there's the story of Roger Laws, of northern Kentucky.

Just downriver from Cincinnati live Roger and his wife Carol. They say they've been UK fans their whole lives. They live on a large tract of land with a big house and an even bigger barn. And that's how it all got started, he says.

"At first I just had a room up in the house," Roger says.

But Carol told him it was unseemly and that he needed to take it out to the barn. She called him a hoarder.

"I really just said that he had so much that he had no room left," Carol says. "He couldn't enjoy it. He needed more room."

"So I thought I might as well," he says. "Turns out I had a *lot* more space in the barn."

It was an old, two-story dairy barn. Now, it's filled from top to bottom with Kentucky basketball memorabilia. It's a museum. There's a regulation-size, full basketball court on the second floor. And in every nook and cranny there's something amazing for UK fans. Autographed jerseys and game-used basketballs and nets go back 60 years.

The Adolph Rupp Trophy, which annually goes to the Player of the Year as voted by Commonwealth Athletic Club of Kentucky, is even housed in this place.

In June 2013, the Lawses invited former UK basketball players to have their annual reunion at the house, with the barn as the centerpiece of the event. More than 30 former players showed up, along with former coach Joe B. Hall. All were amazed by what they saw.

"It's a great place, it sure is," Hall of Fame Player Adrian Smith told the local *Community Recorder* newspaper. "A person to put all of this together—you can tell what a Kentucky fan he is."

"I'm so pleased to be here and be part of it," said UK legend Bob Burrow.

Ed Beck, who played on the 1958 national champions, presented Laws with a gift: the net that was cut down from that championship game.

"It's unbelievable—something you dream about," Laws said of the day. "To have this many people come, to adore Kentucky like I do. It's truly wonderful."

Gerry Calvert, who played at UK from 1954 to 1957, helped organize the event. It was Calvert that dubbed Laws as "Mr. Kentucky No. 1 Fan."

"We all bleed blue," Beck told the crowd. "Always have, always will. We will always remember this day because we gathered here together in this expression of love for UK basketball."

So how do you get to see Roger Laws' barn?

You don't. Unless you're invited. So how do you get an invite?

You get lucky.

In 2014, Joe and I had a book signing at a northern Kentucky sports shop, which was also hosting former UK star Andre Riddick. We had never met Riddick before, but we became fast acquaintances.

A few hundred people showed up to see Riddick, and a few of them even noticed us sitting beside him. Then, an older fellow walked up to Riddick with a backboard sporting what looked to be a hundred autographs—all of former UK stars.

It was Roger Laws. He introduced himself to Riddick, and extended an invitation to come see the barn whenever the UK player had the opportunity. I overheard it, and elbowed Joe. I'd heard of Roger Laws, and his huge memorabilia collection. People talk about those kinds of things. I quickly caught Joe up to speed. When Roger heard that I was interested, he extended the invitation. I was like a kid in *Charlie and the Chocolate Factory*—I had a golden ticket!

The next week, Andre Riddick and I both dropped by Laws' farm. The first thing you notice is imposing metal gates that keep you from getting in. Of course, on top of the gates are wildcats.

Inside the gates, and down a long dirt road, the Lawses' land is littered with animals and structures. The barn is to the left, and outside are just a few clues as to what lay inside.

From trophies to game-used balls and jerseys, Roger Laws' UK memorabilia collection is second to none. His most valuable piece? It could be the actual Rupp trophy, given annually to the nation's top college freshman. Before it makes its way into the hands of a talented player, it is housed here in the Lawses' barn. (Ryan Clark)

Once you step inside, the overall effect is overwhelming. You don't really know what to look at first. There are game balls from the Rupp days. There are championship nets. There are watches and books and glasses and collectibles like nothing you've ever seen. There are famous posters—ones we've all seen where there are little shelves and cabinets filled with UK stuff, like an old Converse shoe. Roger has the *actual shelves of stuff* that the poster featured. They're in glass.

And if that weren't enough, he's got jerseys—actual game-worn jerseys. Laws also has the actual Adolph Rupp Player of the Year trophy. Yes, you read that right.

Upstairs, a full court is decorated with more memorabilia, including a life-size wingspan photo of Anthony Davis, and posters and buttons from previous postseason runs.

Back in the day, there was a Kentucky Basketball Museum just outside Rupp Arena. I'd been several times, and I thought it was awesome, but they just couldn't keep it running—they didn't have the money. Anyway, they had a lot of stuff in the museum. But Roger has more in his barn than any museum I've ever seen. He really does have it all, and it's simply amazing.

So, is there any other way to get in?

"You've got to be invited," Laws says, smiling. "And if you turn me down, you wait one year. Then you may get invited again."

So, if opportunity strikes, for goodness' sake, *don't* turn him down. Say yes. Go. You won't regret it.

—Ryan

Chapter 4

Around the Conference, Around the Country (and Around the World)

You've been around the city, you've been around the state, but let's start running the Big Blue Train on the interstate route...and even the international route. It's time to travel the SEC, from Nashville to Gainesville, Oxford to Athens, Tuscaloosa to two cities named Columbia. From the Ohio UK convention to restaurants and bars around the country to meet fellow Cat fanatics, we've got you covered. And if you really want to broaden your horizons, follow the Cats into another country.

Travel the SEC, and Check out the Cats from a Visitor's Perspective

ince 1932, UK's road to athletic excellence has always wound through the trails of the Southeastern Conference. The SEC was established in December 1932, by thirteen former members of the Southern Conference. Some of the original thirteen have faded away—Sewanee, Tulane, and Georgia Tech were original members of the conference—and others have been added (including Missouri and Texas A&M in 2012), but today, the SEC has become a way of life. ESPN personality and Alabaman Paul Finebaum notably titled his 2014 book *My Conference Can Beat Your Conference*, and in the arms race of college athletics, this has been proved true again and again.

Like cantankerous brothers, the SEC schools and their fans battle each season and rag each other mercilessly 365 days a year. But just let one of their pretentious outsiders from the Big Ten or the Big Twelve or the ACC try to join the conversation. Suddenly the age-old maxim plays out: I can pick on my brother, but if you try it, you're in deep trouble.

Kentucky fandom involves following the team, and each season winds through the highways and byways of the SEC. Here's a hint of what to expect from the other 13 SEC destinations: what to know, where to go, some good places to nab some dinner, and what you can do for fun...besides cheer for (and celebrate) another UK victory.

Nashville, Tennessee (home of **Vanderbilt**, 212 miles from Lexington) was historically the northernmost stop in the SEC aside from Lexington. Since Missouri entered the conference, that has changed. But Vandy, if you can put aside their otherworldly odd arena with benches in the ends of the court, is still a must-see in the SEC.

Nashville is the largest city in the SEC, and there is always plenty to do. Highlights include the Grand Ole Opry, and its former home, the historic Ryman Auditorium, where Hank Williams, Johnny Cash, and others raised hell and sang their songs. Downtown Nashville, complete with the Country Music Hall of Fame, is still a haven for would-be troubadours and those who enjoy a good time.

Historical highlights include the Hermitage, the longtime home of U.S. President Andrew Jackson, and Belle Meade Plantation, a significant stop for Civil War history buffs. For sports fans, the NFL's Titans and NHL's Predators call Nashville home, and usually have plenty of available tickets.

Nashville is also a foodie's paradise. From the Pancake Pantry for all imaginable flavors of a breakfast staple, to Arnold's for meat-and-three-veggie deliciousness, to Noshville for an exceedingly rare New York-style deli in SEC country, Nashville has visitors covered. But if you're eating in Nashville, you absolutely can't miss the city's (in)famous hot chicken. Deep-fried with something akin to fire (but hotter), it's somehow torture and treat wrapped into one. Prince's Hot Chicken Shack is the historic home, but newcomers like Pepperfire, 400 Degrees, and Hattie B's will all light your mouth ablaze.

Three hours east of Nashville is Knoxville, Tennessee (home of **Tennessee**, 172 miles from Lexington), on the edge of the Great Smoky Mountains. Just over an hour south of Middlesboro, Kentucky, Tennessee's Neyland Stadium, with a six-figure seating capacity and the Volunteer Navy floating outside the stadium walls, is one of the great sights of the conference. While a few more wins there would help make Wildcat fans feel at home, the basketball team's Thompson-Boling Arena has been downright chummy over the years for the Wildcats.

Located in east Tennessee, at the confluence of Interstate 75 and Interstate 40, Knoxville's metro population is about 850,000. In addition to the Smokies, which are gorgeous but flanked by tourist traps, there are plenty of memorable sights to enjoy. For the most family inclined, the Women's Basketball Hall of Fame is in Knoxville—hardly surprising since Queen of the Hardwood Pat Summitt made her name coaching the Lady Vols. The Knoxville Zoo is another interesting possibility for the young or young at heart.

While Gatlinburg and Pigeon Forge always present the chance to purchase airbrushed T-shirts, "Old Tyme" photographs, and copious amounts of fudge, much of Knoxville's shopping is in or around West Towne Mall. The city has a variety of good eateries, but the pasta at Louis's, on the north end of town, is always worth seeking out.

Two states over, Columbia, South Carolina (home of **South Carolina**, 410 miles from Lexington), is still a fresh delight to many—having only been an SEC destination since 1992. Columbia is the state's capital, and with a metro population of almost 800,000, the Gamecocks are a superb host.

Cultural highlights of Columbia include an outstanding zoo and a very impressive art museum. They know how to cook in South Carolina, with food options ranging from tasty barbecue to college-standard-fare burger and fries at Rockaway's.

One of the high points of Carolina—particularly as the football game is often played early in the season—is the chance to sneak in a beach trip. Columbia is less than two hours from Charleston and its neighboring Folly Beach, and less than three hours from Myrtle Beach or Hilton Head, just off the coast of Savannah, Georgia. Charleston and Savannah are two of the more interesting Southern cities and either or both will bookend a football weekend nicely for a fun vacation.

Similarly, warm temperatures and relatively nearby beaches are a high point of a trip to Gainesville, Florida (home of **Florida**, 711

SEC HIGHLIGHTS

Closest to Lexington: 1. Knoxville, TN (Tennessee); 2. Nashville, TN (Vanderbilt); 3. Athens, GA (UGA); 4. Columbia, SC (South Carolina); 5. Virtual tie of several cities in the 450–480 mile range

Most interesting for non–sports fans: 1. Nashville, TN (Vanderbilt); 2. Oxford, MS (Ole Miss); 3. Athens, GA (UGA); 4. Baton Rouge, LA (LSU); 5. Too close to call

Best hoops experiences: 1. Fayetteville, AR (Arkansas); 2. Gainesville, FL (Florida); 3. Nashville, TN (Vandy); 4. Knoxville, TN (Tennessee); 5. Columbia, MO (Missouri)

Best football experiences: 1. Baton Rouge, LA (LSU); 2. Tuscaloosa, AL (Alabama); 3. Athens, GA (Georgia); 4. Gainesville, FL (Florida); 5. Knoxville, TN (Tennessee)

Best overall: Too close to rank, but a top five would be (alphabetically listed) Athens, Baton Rouge, Gainesville, Nashville, and Oxford.

miles from Lexington). Ben Hill Griffin Stadium packs more than 85,000 rabid blue-and-orange-clad Gator fans on top of each other on Saturday. It's a boisterous environment, and one in which Kentucky has had little success in recent years.

With around 125,000 people, Gainesville is one of the smaller SEC cities. Located in north central Florida, it's just less than two hours away from the Magic Kingdom, where young children are drawn by what can only be magnetic forces. Jacksonville and Tampa are fairly close, so an NCAA/NFL doubleheader is possible for the lucky sports fan.

There are plenty of fun outdoor events, and good seafood is never more than a long stone's throw away. Despite the recent success of Florida basketball (and the small size of the Gators' O'Connell Center), it's still a relatively easy basketball ticket. Gainesville isn't the most glamorous spot in the SEC, but who can complain about Florida in fall or winter?

By comparison, Athens, Georgia (home of **Georgia**, 380 miles from Lexington), similarly a small city of around 100,000, is one of the most well-rounded SEC destinations. Sanford Stadium, with its historic hedges, has the feel of a college football shrine. That said, Athens has an interesting folksy/artsy vibe that intertwines nicely with face-painted fans in silver britches. UGA gave the world Herschel Walker and the band REM, and both have something distinctly of Athens in their makeup.

Small-business shoppers will love Athens' impressive array of local shops, particularly prevalent on Clayton Street downtown. A multitude of excellent eateries are available. From Weaver D's, where REM used to enjoy meat-and-three standards, to the Last Resort, which is famous for a fried-green-tomato sandwich, your wallet may be the only thing that doesn't do well in Athens.

Walking tours highlight both the town's history and its musical connections—aside from Michael Stipe and company, the B-52s, Matthew Sweet, and the Drive-By Truckers are just a few of the many musicians affiliated with Athens. To summarize, the Georgians know how to play, how to eat and drink, and how to enjoy some football. Dominique Wilkins aside, they're still catching up in the roundball.

Columbia, Missouri (home of **Missouri**, 460 miles from Lexington) is one of the new kids on the SEC block. Another city of around 100,000, way out in central Missouri, it's too early to have much of an opinion of the city as an SEC destination. It does sit halfway between Kansas City and St. Louis, so like the other Columbia, it's a good midpoint destination. Booches has an allegedly famous burger, and being able to enjoy Thai food by the side of the Missouri River probably makes Chim's Thai Kitchen a must visit.

Similarly, College Station, Texas (home of **Texas A&M**, 981 miles from Lexington), is a new SEC destination. At around an hour from Houston and not quite two hours from Austin, an A&M road trip is a great excuse to see the Lone Star state. Beyond that, well, it may take a few years to assess the situation. In the meanwhile, how can you go wrong with Texas barbecue? C&J Barbeque market serves fresh Texas brisket and jalapeno sausage.

Fayetteville, Arkansas (home of **Arkansas**, 671 miles from Lexington), has only been an SEC site for two decades or so, but is one of the best basketball environments in the conference. The Razorbacks haven't quite returned to the level of success they had under Nolan Richardson, but Walton Arena is a memorable spot to enjoy a game. Reynolds Stadium in Fayetteville is very nice, and neighboring War Memorial Stadium in Little Rock (which gets a game or two per season) has been relatively kind to the football Cats, but as an SEC West foe, those trips are fairly rare.

It's a long haul out to northwest Arkansas, but outdoorsy types will enjoy the neighboring Ozarks. Fayetteville is also often cited as one of the best barbecue spots in America, with geography bringing together the Memphis and Texas 'cue traditions. You can't go wrong at places like the Whole Hog Café or Herman's, where the ribs are probably even more of an Arkansas institution than Wal-Mart (locally headquartered).

Perhaps the most glamorous SEC West venue is down on the bayou at Baton Rouge, Louisiana (home of **LSU**, 764 miles from Lexington). A mere hour and a half from New Orleans, Baton Rouge is a must see, not only for the unique cultural aspects of the area, but also for the raucous atmosphere around LSU sports. Tiger Stadium is one of the loudest and wildest environments in the nation. It hasn't been kind to the Cats, or much of anybody else for that matter. That said, it's intense, passionate, and a thrilling must-see.

LSU roundball has been up and down, but the very fact that games go on in the Maravich Center tells you that this is basketball country.

UK's stunning 31-point comeback win over the Tigers took place here in 1994, and they still haven't recovered.

Tailgating at LSU is hardcore—and that aside, there's tons to do. Swamp tours are a must and the city zoo is affordable. For that matter, the state capitol is an interesting spot for history buffs—as the great Senator Huey Long was shot down there in 1935. And dining— oh, the dining. From the Chimes (an LSU favorite, with a lot of the usual Cajun favorites) to carry-out spots like Jerry Lee's Kwik Stop or the near-campus Zeeland Street Market, it's an embarrassment of riches. By the time you're finished, you'll never want to geaux back home.

Another SEC staple is Oxford, Mississippi (home of **Ole Miss**, 470 miles from Lexington). Oxford is a small town about an hour outside of Memphis, and it is quirky and historic. Nobel Prize winner William Faulkner called the place home, and for a few dollars you can still tour his home, Rowan Oak, where the outline of his novel *A Fable* survives written on a wall. Modern best-seller John Grisham is from Oxford, as are many, many other great writers. There's a fun and eclectic live music scene as well, which is well worth checking out. Most of Oxford centers around the downtown square, with the unparalleled Square Books boasting not one, not two, but three separate shops within a stone's throw.

Ole Miss is in the process of building a new basketball arena, which is a welcome decision. The football stadium, Vaught-Hemingway, is one of the smaller stadiums in the conference, and is very intimate and enjoyable. But the real tradition here is the Grove, a large rectangle in the middle of Ole Miss's campus that is tailgating central. As the locals say, "We might lose the game, but we have never lost a party." And they're right.

Elvis fans can craft a great road trip with Oxford involved, as Memphis is an hour north, with Sun Studios and Graceland to visit, and Tupelo, with Elvis' birthplace and childhood home, is an hour east. If you're not a huge fan of the King, then spend the extra time eating in Oxford. Taylor Grocery, a few miles out of town, has the best catfish in the history of the universe. City Grocery is white-tableclothed excellence, and the Beacon is the kind of breakfast sanctuary that every town should have.

On the other hand, Starkville, Mississippi (home of **Mississippi State**, 468 miles from Lexington), is probably the sleepiest town in the SEC. Johnny Cash wrote a song called "Starkville City Jail" when he was arrested for public drunkenness. The city turned the event into a festival recently, and posthumously pardoned the Man in Black.

Bulldog basketball has been pretty dozy in recent seasons as well, but the Humphrey Coliseum (aka "The Hump") can get wild when the Dogs give their fans reason to cheer. Davis-Wade Stadium is the home of some clanging cowbells, but as MSU is UK's permanent SEC West opponent, you might as well get used to them. Most State fans are pretty gracious, and if they're not, after the ubiquitous cowbells, you can't hear the difference. Baseball is perhaps MSU's best sport, and Polk-Dement Stadium is worth checking out for hardball fans.

A short drive east can end up in Tuscaloosa, Alabama (home of **Alabama**, 459 miles from Lexington), where the Crimson Tide have made football dominance an art form—so much of an art form, in fact, that the Bear Bryant Museum, on Alabama's campus, gives the subject proper treatment. Complete with a Hall of Honor and a replica of Bryant's office, the museum is a must see, even if 'Bama fans might need to be reminded that the Bear's SEC beginnings came in Lexington, not Tuscaloosa.

Bryant-Denny Stadium seats more than 100,000, and will still prove to be one of the tougher tickets in the SEC. Of course, Alabama isn't the SEC's football king for no reason. It's a must-see. In an equally fine tradition, Mercedes-Benz produces cars in Tuscaloosa, and for the automotively inclined, a factory tour is a fun stop.

If you're looking for eats, Dreamland BBQ does for ribs what Saban, Bryant, et al. do for the gridiron. If you miss it, you'll wish you hadn't. The Houndstooth is one of many spots in town to obtain a libation, but like most college towns, you won't lack for food or drink.

East of Tuscaloosa, not as flashy, but just as memorable, Auburn, Alabama (home of **Auburn**, 465 miles from Lexington), claims the moniker of "The Loveliest Village on the Plains." While the Tigers can't quite match the cross-state Tide in sports history, they have their own sports museum on campus, again mostly with a football focus…although basketball great Charles Barkley was an Auburn Tiger as well, among many others.

Jordan-Hare Stadium remains one of the SEC's best football venues, and with hard times in basketball, Auburn Arena has been an easy spot for Cat fans to invade—although coach Bruce Pearl doubtlessly plans to change that. One part of Auburn tradition that is sadly gone is Toomer's Corner, where Tiger fans "rolled" famous trees with toilet paper after Auburn victories, until an Alabama fan poisoned the trees in 2011.

Nearby Toomer Drugs is alive and well, and worth a visit for a homemade lemonade. Stronger drink can be found at the War Eagle Supper Club. An impressive art museum and multiple local golf courses are among the other Auburn highlights.

EXTRA POINTS

Cat Trackers

For decades, Kentucky fan Jan Pfeffer organized trips taking UK supporters across the world.

The name of their group? The Cat Trackers. No game seemed out of reach, and bad weather be damned. The Trackers would pile on to a bus and head out. New York. The SEC Tourney. Hawaii. No trip was out of the question. Sadly, in the fall of 2014, Pfeffer passed away of a heart attack at age 80.

"She was always young at heart," says friend Jim Porter. And her legacy will live on, because the co-founder of Cat Trackers, Rita Dunham, has pledged to continue the trips. (Interested? Email her at ldunham7514@fuse.net.)

Visit the Ohio UK Convention

WHERE: Eastview Baptist Church, Franklin, Ohio (4289 W. State Route 122)

WHEN: On a Saturday in July—watch Larry Vaught's column or www.ukconvention.com for details

HOW TO DO IT: Convention director Jim Porter has an open door policy. There is a fee for participating, but that's the only known requirement, other than Kentucky fandom.

COST FACTOR: $$, $25 entry fee, which covers the cost of the event and earns a "door prize"

DIFFICULTY FACTOR: ▮

BUCKET RANK: 🗑 🗑 🗑

HINTS FOR LITTLE WILDCATS/RELUCTANT WILDCATS: The convention is mostly geared toward older folks, but is very much family appropriate.

Twenty-five years ago, Jim Porter had a dream. Well, not a literal dream. But Porter, an uber UK fan living in Franklin, Ohio, wanted to cheer up a sick pal and fellow Wildcat backer. He set up shop at a local state park, invited a few friends, and asked Wildcat Shelby Linville to give a brief talk.

A quarter century later, Porter's friendly get-together has become a tradition. Former Wildcat legends, local media members, and UK staffers all converge with an ever-growing crowd of Wildcat backers on Eastview Baptist Church in Franklin, where the sanctuary is given over from worship to Big Blue fandom.

I had heard of the convention from years prior. It had become semi-famous after guest speaker Jeff Sheppard had been somewhat critical of the one-and-done system in the 2011 convention. But in 2014, I

EXTRA POINTS

Mom's Restaurant

Among the many pleasant moments of the convention is a chance to break for lunch at Mom's Restaurant. Mom's (1111 William C Good Boulevard, Franklin, Ohio) sits in the side of a gas station, and at first glance, just blends into the scenery. But don't be fooled—Hilda Ratliff and her crew are serving up some serious home-cooked goodness and showing support for the Kentucky Wildcats.

But first, what's with the name? Well, Hilda became "Mom" to a group of local cops who frequented the restaurant when it was in a somewhat less desirable location. Hilda says the officers would stow their mugs at the restaurant awaiting their next coffee fill-up—and if you stop by Mom's, you might wish you had a waiting mug as well.

Mom's is appropriately decked out in blue and white, with pictures and memorabilia all over the restaurant. I assumed at first that Hilda's UK fandom might have been the result of some prodding from Mr. Porter. But the truth goes much deeper. UK football star Doug Pelfrey was one of the locals who helped relocate Mom's to its current location, and Hilda's blood runs true blue.

Lunch is great—open-faced roast beef sandwiches, meatloaf, and other comfort food abounds, but breakfast might be where Mom's really raises the bar. Scrambled eggs, fresh sausage, homemade biscuits and blue gravy…wait, *what*?

Yes, the unequivocal highlight of Mom's has to be her *blue* gravy. For a true-blue Kentucky fan, what could be a more natural fit? It's not always available, but great food always is. Mr. Porter drops by when he can, and you're assured of some pleasant, down-home dining at Mom's, which has somehow moved Big Blue Country a few miles north.

got to enjoy the event first hand. Porter had brought together a group of dedicated, mostly older Wildcat fans, covering several states. One attendee shared memories of hitchhiking to watch Ralph Beard and Wah Wah Jones play in the KHSAA state tournament. A 92-year-old gentleman, who won an award for oldest attendee, recounted as a key to his longevity that he had avoided hard liquor—but laughingly admitted that he did enjoy beer. Stories were swapped, laughs were enjoyed, and I won a UK seat cushion for my door prize.

In 2014, Jack Givens was a featured speaker, and he covered a variety of interesting topics. From one-and-dones (Givens said he'd rather have them on his team than play against them) to cookies (he appreciated the fresh ones he was frequently given in his NBA career by UK backers), no subject was out of bounds. His stories about Joe B. Hall were worth the $25 entry fee alone.

Other speakers included UK senior associate athletic director for compliance Rachel Baker, who held up well when asked to explain a multitude of NCAA misdeeds (Baker is a former NCAA employee). Also in attendance and leading discussion were Kentucky Sports Radio's Ryan Lemond, CatsPause.com recruiting guru Josh Edwards, and Danville newspaper columnist Larry Vaught.

Jim Porter was everywhere at the convention, and his affable good humor kept the day moving. Whether he was joking that the convention was the equivalent of six hours' credit in UK studies, or was leading a silent auction of an impressive array of memorabilia and sometimes homemade artifacts, Porter was the head honcho. He has created an enjoyable UK weekend—particularly so for those who are dislocated Cat fans like himself. At the pace that Porter is moving, in another twenty-five years, he may need an arena to house the convention.

Check out Future Cats in All-Star Showdowns

WHERE: The locations rotate in the Kentucky–Indiana basketball series, and in football, the game has settled in Williamsburg, Kentucky

WHEN: The football game takes place in January, and the basketball series is a mid-year event.

HOW TO DO IT: Just go and enjoy!

COST FACTOR: $$ per ticket

DIFFICULTY FACTOR: █ As crowds dwindle, this gets easier and easier

BUCKET RANK: 🗑 🗑

HINTS FOR LITTLE WILDCATS/RELUCTANT WILDCATS: Not much else to do on this one. The girls basketball series with Indiana has been more competitive than the boys game in recent years, and tends to feature as many, if not more, future stars.

For the past 75 years, a group of Kentucky's elite high school basketball players have faced off against Indiana's top high schoolers in a series for pride and charity. The Lions Club and its eye-related charities are the beneficiaries of the Kentucky–Indiana All-Star Classic series, but any Wildcat fan that is lucky enough to catch a future UK star recognizes the relevance of this game.

It is the longest-running annual all-star game of its kind. The two teams play twice annually, once in Kentucky and once in Indiana, in a battle for bragging rights. Among the legendary Wildcats who showed their skills in the series are Ralph Beard, Frank Ramsey, Larry Conley, Darius Miller, and Dominique Hawkins. Of course, Wildcats don't only suit up on the Kentucky side. In 2011, soon-to-be UK point guard Marquis Teague drained a shot in the final seconds to push Indiana past Kentucky 105–103. Trey Lyles was chosen for the Indiana team in 2014, but was unable to play due to illness.

Additionally, Matthew Mitchell's Kentucky hoops squad is often prominently featured in the girls' version of the games. Miss Basketball A'dia Mathies led the 2009 Kentucky squad, and Makayla Epps starred for the 2013 team. The games also tend to showcase other talented stars, including such luminaries as Tennessee's Allan Houston and Chris Lofton, and Western Kentucky's Clem Haskins and Jim McDaniels.

If the gridiron is your thing, then it's the Kentucky–Tennessee All-Star Game. That annual series began in 1984, and annually flipped between UT's campus in Knoxville and Kentucky's in Lexington. In 2007, that format ended, and the game became the National Guard Border Bowl, with a permanent home in Williamsburg, Kentucky.

Many Wildcats have found glory in this gridiron rivalry. In 1996, All-World QB Tim Couch led Kentucky to a 10–0 win, snapping a six-game Tennessee winning streak. Couch not only led the Kentucky offense, but also punted for the all-star team. Future UK quarterback Jared Lorenzen was not as lucky in 1999, as he came up just short in a 9–7 heartbreaker. In recent years, UK players such as Zach West, Darrian Miller, and Jacob Hyde have taken part in the Border Bowl. In any given year, Cat fans can get a good preview of outstanding collegiate talent during what would normally be football's offseason. By any name, that's a recipe for success.

Burger Boys

Under John Calipari, Kentucky's all-star game of choice has become the McDonald's All-American Game. The premier showcase for all-star high school talent, that game, while played across the nation, has at least become must-see TV for UK backers.

The full list of UK McDonald's alumni is:

Dwight Anderson (1978)
Clarence Tillman (1978)
Chuck Verderber (1978)
Sam Bowie (1979)
Derrick Hord (1979)
Dirk Minniefield (1979)
Bret Bearup (1980)
Jim Master (1980)
Roger Harden (1982)
Kenny Walker (1982)
Winston Bennett (1983)
James Blackmon (1983)
Ed Davender (1984)
Cedric Jenkins (1984)
Richard Madison (1984)
Irving Thomas (1985)
Rex Chapman (1986)
Eric Manuel (1987)
Chris Mills (1988)
Tony Delk (1992)
Rodrick Rhodes (1992)
Antoine Walker (1994)
Ron Mercer (1995)
Wayne Turner (1995)
Tayshaun Prince (1998)
Keith Bogans (1999)
Marvin Stone (1999)

Rashaad Carruth (2001)
Joe Crawford (2004)
Randolph Morris (2004)
Rajon Rondo (2004)
Patrick Patterson (2007)
DeMarcus Cousins (2009)
Terrence Jones (2010)
Brandon Knight (2010)
Doron Lamb (2010)
Anthony Davis (2011)
Michael Kidd-Gilchrist (2011)
Marquis Teague (2011)
Kyle Wiltjer (2011)
Archie Goodwin (2012)
Alex Poythress (2012)
Aaron Harrison (2013)
Andrew Harrison (2013)
Dakari Johnson (2013)
Marcus Lee (2013)
Julius Randle (2013)
James Young (2013)
Devin Booker (2014)
Trey Lyles (2014)
Karl-Anthony Towns (2014)
Tyler Ulis (2014)
Isaiah Briscoe (2015)

UK Hoops:

Jennifer O'Neill (2010)
Bria Goss (2011)
Janee Thompson (2012)
Makayla Epps (2013)
Linnae Harper (2013)
Alyssa Rice (2014)
Taylor Murray (2015)

Alex Poythress, from Clarksville, Tennessee, was a McDonald's All-American before coming to play at Kentucky. In 2014–15, he was one of a record nine such All-Americans to play on one team. (Duke also had nine that season.) (Tim Sofranko)

See the Hoops Vols Get Knocked off Rocky Top: Kentucky vs. Tennessee

WHERE: Usually Lexington or Knoxville, although the occasional SEC Tournament meeting isn't unusual either

WHEN: In days of yore, a home-and-home series occurred every year. These days, the schools play every year, but not necessarily twice. The game(s) will be in January or February.

HOW TO DO IT: Not a particularly tough ticket, and given the size of UT's Thompson-Boling Arena, a very viable road ticket

COST FACTOR: Sometimes as cheap as $$ per ticket, and $$$ should yield a good spot

DIFFICULTY FACTOR: ▌ Although possibly ▌ depending on whether Tennessee is any good in a given year

BUCKET RANK: 🗑🗑🗑🗑

HINTS FOR LITTLE WILDCATS/RELUCTANT WILDCATS:
Knoxville is a short jaunt from both the Smokey Mountains and the Blue Ridge Mountains. It makes a nice road trip, particularly when coupled with an almost-inevitable win.

S ome favor Indiana as UK's most despised rival. Others contend that it's Louisville. Based on its success and holier-than-thou mannerisms, Duke is also a favorite in the conversation. But I disagree with all of these. The enemy wears blazing orange, and not just because he got lost on an overlong hunting trip. He is represented by a bumpkin with a musket and a hat like Cousin Eddie from *Christmas Vacation*. Either that or a big, slobbery dog, despite the fact that their team mascot has nothing to do with dogs in any fashion. He knows every word to "Rocky Top," and sings it proudly, even though it celebrates people so backward that they are more intimately familiar with moonshine stills than telephones.

But don't misunderstand. Thank goodness for the Tennessee Volunteers. Yes, you did read that right. Without the Vols, UK would be fourth all-time in most NCAA wins. There are at least 151 separate reasons (as of the beginning of the 2015–16 season) to be grateful for UT, if we count each Kentucky victory over its border-state neighbors. And the harsh truth is that while UK has the most wins all-time over UT, it has more losses to UT than any other school as well.

In truth, Tennessee fans, when you can get them to stop singing "Rocky Top," actually tend to have an appreciation of the Kentucky basketball dynasty. Volunteer football, despite its recent struggles, is a perennial national power, and UT football tends to view Kentucky football in the same light as Wildcat backers know UT hoops. While Tennessee has never made a Final Four, the school has produced Ray Mears, Ernie (Grunfeld) and Bernie (King), Allan Houston, Bruce Pearl, Chris Lofton, and a host of memorable matchups with Kentucky. And while UT can be chastised for its NCAA transgressions, it is worth remembering (as Adolph Rupp famously *did*) that when the rest of the SEC voted to cancel UK's season after the 1951 point-shaving scandal, only UT voted to keep UK's SEC schedule intact. Tennessee fans respect passion, and that has certainly helped the border war between the two states.

All of that said, lest anyone think I'm getting too soft on the Vols, when I make my list of most loathed opposing players, there are always plenty of Vols on the list. Tiny Tony Harris with his yapping mouth and ready fists, Ron Slay and his oversized headband, Hopkinsville, Kentucky's king of trash talk Scotty Hopson, and

ROCKY TOP THIS!

A top five of unforgettable UK/UT basketball moments:

1. **January 13, 2009**: In what was unquestionably the best moment of the Billy Gillispie era, Jodie Meeks led UK in a 90–72 beatdown of No. 24 Tennessee. Meeks set the UK single-game scoring record, putting up 54 points on 15-for-22 shooting (10-for-15 on threes, 14-of-14 on free throws) and leaving every Tennessee fan in Thompson-Boling Arena muttering to him- or herself. The man was automatic.

2. **That decade when UK didn't lose to UT**: Yes, from February 1950 to January 1960, Kentucky owned the series, winning 20 games in a row, with half of the wins being by 25 or more.

3. **February 11, 1987**: Tennessee thought they had stolen a win in Rupp Arena when they held a 10-point lead with 1:13 to play. Fortunately, Rex Chapman and the Cats had other ideas, delivering an amazing comeback to tie the game and surge to a 91–84 overtime win.

4. **March 12, 1993**: Two weeks after UT stole a win in Knoxville over UK 78–77 (and yes, *stole* is the operative word, as the key basket in the win was scored on an offensive rebound off of a blatant UT lane violation), UK avenged itself. The game is remembered less for the 101–40 margin than for the fact that UK 13th man Todd Svoboda outscored UT All-American Allan Houston. In fact, UT was so awful that in his seven minutes of play, Svoboda also grabbed more rebounds than any UT player did in the game, and he also would've tied for team-high honors in assists for the Vols. As an

aside, a bridge just across the Tennessee state line from my house was boldly painted "101–40" for years thereafter. I had nothing to do with it, I almost swear.

5. **March 13, 2010:** In what became Bruce Pearl's final SEC game, UK delivered an SEC semifinal beatdown 74–45 over the No. 15 Vols. The game featured four technical fouls, as the frustrated Vols showed their thuggish true colors. For UK, freshmen DeMarcus Cousins, Eric Bledsoe, and John Wall combined for 50 points.

even solid citizens like Chris Lofton and Allan Houston are among the players I most enjoyed seeing shut down by their opponents in blue and white. But whenever I get too angry, I reflect on those 151 wins. If Louisville is Kentucky's little brother, Tennessee must be the orange-headed stepbrother.

There is one story that perhaps better than the others, sums up the relationship. The story circulates so widely that it might be apocryphal, but the *Baltimore Sun* told it in 1997, so it must be true. The story goes that in the months after UK's 101–40 beating of UT in 1993, Rick Pitino was having a conversation with highly regarded recruit Ron Mercer, a native of Tennessee. Mercer confessed to Pitino that Tennessee was his other final school of choice. Pitino asked Mercer if he remembered UT star Allan Houston. Yes, Mercer admitted; in fact, Houston was one of his favorite players. Pitino next asked if he remembered how UK had handled Houston in the 101-40 blowout. Mercer recalled that the UT star was held to just three points. "If you go to Tennessee," Pitino half-joked and half-threatened, "we'll do the same thing to you." Mercer got the point. He chose UK, won a national title, became an NBA lottery pick, and never looked back.

—Joe

Watch the Football Cats in a Bowl Game

WHERE: Given the paucity of bowl games, almost anywhere, although Nashville is the most popular recent destination

WHEN: Late December–early January, provided the team can string six-plus wins together

HOW TO DO IT: Season ticket holders get first crack, but for most UK bowl games, there are plenty of available seats via even the most mundane of channels (Ticketmaster, Stubhub, etc.).

COST FACTOR: $$+

DIFFICULTY FACTOR: ▌ Most years, the hard part is the team reaching the game

BUCKET RANK: 🗑 🗑 🗑 🗑

HINTS FOR LITTLE WILDCATS/RELUCTANT WILDCATS: Bowl games are usually in warm weather locales near the holidays. Provided your significant other and/or kids don't mind some relatively chilly weather, it's a good time for all!

O n December 6, 1947, UK played Villanova in the first and last Great Lakes Bowl. A few hardy Wildcat fans were treated to a 24–14 win in the freezing confines of Cleveland Stadium. The good news is that every UK Wildcat bowl appearance since then has been in much more pleasant weather. The bad news is that there have only been 14 more bowl appearances in nearly seven decades.

In the modern college football climate, six wins for UK equals a bowl trip. While most of the Wildcats' recent success has come in the lower-tier bowl games, any excuse to get out of town, play another football game, and win an accolade makes a Wildcat bowl appearance a must see. Most bowl games involve plenty of fun and pageantry and make a fine excuse for a winter minivacation.

That said, the good, the bad, and the ugly are all very much a part of UK's bowl history. In 1993, the Big Blue Nation watched as UK's hard-charging linebacker Marty Moore made a late interception that appeared to clinch a Peach Bowl win—until Moore fumbled the ball right back to Clemson, which promptly scored a touchdown, as UK grabbed defeat from the jaws of victory 14–13.

On a more personal level, in 1999, both of your humble authors watched the Cats play in the Music City Bowl in Nashville. The game was relatively new, and this was only UK's fifth bowl appearance in our respective lifetimes. UK marched up and down the field to begin the game, jumping out to a 10–0 lead over Syracuse before Wildcat All-American tight end James Whalen suffered a horrific arm injury. UK was never the same, and eventually lost the game 20–13.

That said, from the "getting there is half the fun" department, I had only begun my day of misery. I drove home from the game, and somewhere in northeast Tennessee, I started having car trouble. My dashboard looked like the panel of an airplane that was urgently trying to tell me that it was about to crash. I drove on, apparently weaving badly enough that I drew the attention of local law enforcement. A day that began with hopes of UK football glory ended with my being given field sobriety tests by a Tennessee cop as I tried to explain that the problem was purely vehicular. After I recited the alphabet backward, I was allowed to go on my way. I seem to recall a *Deliverance*-like warning to stay out of them there parts, but hopefully, that is embellishment.

In 2006, the Wildcats' run without a bowl win was old enough to vote and drink. So when UK surprised everyone with a 7–5

UK WILDCATS IN BOWL GAMES

Season	Bowl Game	Outcome
1947	Great Lakes Bowl (Cleveland, OH)	UK 24, Villanova 14
1949	Orange Bowl (Miami, FL)	Santa Clara 21, UK 13
1950	Sugar Bowl (New Orleans, LA)	UK 13, Oklahoma 7
1951	Cotton Bowl (Dallas, TX)	UK 20, TCU 7
1976	Peach Bowl (Atlanta, GA)	UK 21, North Carolina 0
1983	Hall of Fame Bowl (Birmingham, AL)	West Virginia 20, UK 16
1984	Hall of Fame Bowl (Birmingham, AL)	UK 20, Wisconsin 19
1993	Peach Bowl (Atlanta, GA)	Clemson 14, UK 13
1998	Outback Bowl (Tampa, FL)	Penn State 26, UK 14
1999	Music City Bowl (Nashville, TN)	Syracuse 20, UK 13
2006	Music City Bowl (Nashville, TN)	UK 28, Clemson 20
2007	Music City Bowl (Nashville, TN)	UK 35, Florida State 28
2008	Liberty Bowl (Memphis, TN)	UK 29, East Carolina 19
2009	Music City Bowl (Nashville, TN)	Clemson 21, UK 13
2010	BBVA Compass Bowl (Birmingham, AL)	Pittsburgh 27, UK 10

campaign, my wife and I headed south—back to LP Field for another Music City Bowl. UK was a 10½-point underdog against a talented Clemson team, led by future NFL star C.J. Spiller.

But for one glorious afternoon, UK, led by coach Rich Brooks, went for the kill. The Cats' first touchdown was scored by linebacker Micah Johnson, who was in the game as a running back. But the second was the moment that will live in my memory. UK, holding a tenuous 7–6 lead late in the first half, ran a fake punt deep in their own territory. UK punter Tim Masthay completed a short pass to defensive back Marcus McClinton for a stunning first down. On the next play, UK quarterback Andre Woodson sold a play-fake and threw a bomb for receiver Demareo Ford. Ford caught the ball, and finished a 70-yard scoring jaunt. The play unfolded in front of me, and as my wife and I excitedly celebrated, the entire upper deck of LP Field was actually swaying under the weight of Wildcat pandemonium. UK won 28–20, and all was right with the world, at least for a few hours.

Expect the unexpected. But then, that's always been UK football. Hopefully the next bowl trip is the best one yet.

—Joe

Catch the SEC Tournament

WHERE: While it has historically been on a rotating basis, it will be in Nashville at the Bridgestone Arena annually through at least 2025, with the exceptions of 2018 (St. Louis) and 2022 (Tampa).

WHEN: Annually in early-to-mid-March

HOW TO DO IT: Well, the tickets are the hard part. That said, I spoke with a friend who indicated that he, his father, and his son had all attended the tournament, at a price about 25 percent over the face value of the book of tickets. The time-honored strategy is to latch on to a fan base from a school with a terrible team and buy tickets from their disappointed exiting fans. The problem is that there are fewer and fewer such fans, and more and more demand for the tickets.

COST FACTOR: Generally $$$, although if you want a great seat, particularly for the whole tournament, it's more along the lines of $$$$

DIFFICULTY FACTOR: ▮ based on the high demand for tickets. Buy ahead or prepare to pay.

BUCKET RANK: 🗑️ 🗑️ 🗑️ 🗑️

HINTS FOR LITTLE WILDCATS/RELUCTANT WILDCATS: Nashville is your friend. While you got a thumbnail sketch in the "Travel the SEC" section, even more info follows. If you're going to spend the better part of a week in a place, you need some recreation.

John Calipari hates it. If it were up to him, there would be no SEC Tournament. He's said it time after time after time. That said, it's Kentucky. Calipari knows that the Big Blue Nation will invade Nashville every spring, and that tax refunds, vacation savings, and 401(k) withdrawals are not spent to see a loss. Still, for the guy who has had an easier time getting to the Final Four than winning the SEC Tournament championship, it's a hard sell.

The good news is that Coach Cal is perhaps the only one for whom the SEC Tournament is a hard sell. Now set more or less annually in Nashville, it's a short trip down I-65 to sit in an arena 90 percent full of Cat fans and enjoy five days of college basketball.

Given the current scheduling format, the top four SEC squads aren't in action until Friday, so those who are less-than-hardcore fans might postpone their arrival until then. But why miss two extra days in Nashville, aside from the difficulty of parting with so many green pictures of dead presidents? Here are a few more great sights, sounds, and tastes to enjoy doing the lead up to the biggest games.

Arena Area

- The Johnny Cash Museum (119 3rd Avenue South) is a short walk from the arena, and a great place to learn a little more about the Man in Black. Cash scholar Bill Miller has tracked it all down, and preserved it in a cool spot to browse and shop.

- If your tastes run more toward Jack White than the Man in Black, check out White's Third Man Records shop (623 7th Avenue South). It even has a recording booth (as utilized by Neil Young on *The Tonight Show with Jimmy Fallon*) where, for a few bucks, you can record your own slab of Nashville twang. Maybe an ode to the Cats?

- For that matter, Broadway (the street where Bridgestone Arena is located) as a whole is the epicenter of Music City. Ernest Tubb's Record Shop (417 Broadway) is one of the best country stores in the world.

- The local drinks-and-food scene downtown is phenomenal. Whether it's modern honky-tonk-scene like Wildhorse Saloon (120 2nd Avenue North) or "Are you sure Hank did it this way?" drop-ins like Tootsie's Orchid Lounge (422 Broadway), there's always a party or twelve.

EXTRA POINTS

Great UK Moments in the SEC Tournament

1. 2010: DeMarcus Cousins beat the buzzer for a tip-in to send the championship game to overtime. In the extra session, John Wall dominated as UK won 75–74. Still, the overarching image of the game is Cousins being mobbed by his teammates after his tip-in.

2. 1995: Kentucky battled back from a 22-point deficit to take mighty Arkansas to overtime. Still, when Rod Rhodes missed two free throws at the end of regulation, and Arkansas went up eight in overtime, things were dim for UK. But Antoine Walker rallied the Cats, and Anthony Epps' clutch free throws gave UK a lead it never relinquished in the 95–93 win.

3. 1992: Jamal Mashburn took the team on his back and delivered an SEC championship to the Unforgettables. As UK had been banned for two seasons from tournament play, this was an extra-special 80–54 win over Alabama.

4. 1984: Kenny Walker made a short jumper just ahead of the buzzer to upend Auburn 51–49, for UK's first SEC Tournament title since the league reinstated the tournament. Auburn senior Charles Barkley sat on the floor and wept like a baby.

5. 2003: A 64–57 title win over Mississippi State was the icing on the cake of a 19–0 SEC season for Tubby Smith's Wildcats. The team lost in the Elite Eight to Marquette, but a perfect SEC season is a rare feat.

Out in Town

- Green Hills is Nashville's prime shopping area. While the mall is typical corporate fare, there are cool places aplenty—for books, try Parnassus (3900 Hillsboro Pike) and for open-mic genius, the world-famous Bluebird Café (4104 Hillsboro Pike) is all that it should be. Make reservations for the latter, and you'll be glad you did.

- If you want to stretch your legs, check out the Parthenon (2500 West End Avenue). Yes, like the Greek one. A full-scale replica, built in 1897, this Parthenon lies in a park area, with plenty of room to stroll or pig out from the food trucks.

- Close to the Parthenon is the Belcourt Theatre (2102 Belcourt Avenue), where indie films and classic movies play. The Belcourt was the temporary home of the Grand Ole Opry during World War II, and that entire area is full of crafty local shops, for those who enjoy such things.

- Nashville restaurants could (and probably do) have their own book. A few more recommendations: Monell's (now three locations) for family style home cooking, The Loveless Café (8400 Tennessee Highway 100) for the genuine version of what Cracker Barrel is trying to impart, and Arnold's (605 8th Avenue South) for meat-and-three heaven. And two more—I know it's a repeat sermon, but get some Nashville hot chicken or you'll wish you had. And check out Las Paletas (2911 12th Avenue South) for a cool, tasty snack of popsicles made from real fruit.

- I would be remiss if I didn't mention the Opry Mills area. I'd echo Yogi Berra on this one and advise you, "Nobody goes there anymore. It's too crowded." But if you like outlet malls and a gigantic hotel, give it a go.

Back to the basketball, or more accurately, the official SEC distraction. SEC Fan Fare, located in front of the Country Music Hall of Fame at 5th and Demonbreun, is the SEC's attempt to spread the party. Live music, SEC legends, interactive games, and lots of fun are promised.

Inside the arena, the real business takes place. Quarterfinals are on Friday, semifinals are on Saturday, and the championship game is on selection Sunday. So after you've people watched and shopped and enjoyed Nashville, it's time to settle in and cheer for the Cats.

Over the years, it's fair to say that Kentucky has done pretty well in the SEC Tournament. The all-time score is UK 28, the entire rest of the SEC, including past members, 27. The tournament was played annually from 1933 to 1952, with the 1941–52 tourneys taking place in the Louisville Gardens. After the 1952–53 "lost season" for UK due to NCAA probation, the tournament did not occur again until 1979, whence it has continued until the present day.

. . . .

Follow Your Favorite Cats in the NBA

Jack Givens liked cookies. He knew it and his teammates knew it, but much to their amazement, in virtually any city that his Atlanta Hawks visited, a Wildcat fan knew it—and made sure that "The Goose" had plenty of his favorite snacks. Three decades later, Givens still remembers the cookies. He laughingly recalls his teammates' excitement over the Wildcat fans who invariably showed up and brought Givens (and, because he was a nice guy, his teammates) sweet treats. His audience at the Ohio UK Convention understood. Probably some of them had baked the cookies. There is life in the NBA, and there is life in the NBA as a Kentucky Wildcat.

Accepting as a given that Kentucky fans are among the most passionate in the nation, if not the universe, and as approximately a tenth of the current NBA is made up of former Kentucky players, then it logically follows that a Big Blue must is to follow your favorite Wildcat legends in the NBA careers.

While the list of Wildcats in the league changes literally day to day, there are a few mainstays who should be league fixtures for years to come. 2012 NCAA Player of the Year Anthony Davis of the New Orleans Pelicans has rapidly become one of the most talented and productive players in the league. 2010 Wildcats John Wall and DeMarcus Cousins both were chosen for the 2015 NBA All-Star Game, and have made the Wizards and Kings, two usually putrid squads, competitive in their respective divisions.

Rajon Rondo played two years at UK under Tubby Smith, but his skills ultimately shone as a Boston Celtic, where he became an NBA champion and a four-time All-Star. A few of the other most popular Wildcats in the NBA include Eric Bledsoe, Terrence Jones, Michael Kidd-Gilchrist, Brandon Knight, and Nerlens Noel. As the 2015 season wound down, it was harder to find an NBA team without a Wildcat than a team with one. One team, the Phoenix Suns, had no fewer than three UK players—Bledsoe, Knight, and Archie Goodwin—and that was before they drafted former Cat Devin Booker.

EXTRA POINTS

A Few All-Time Great UK Pros

Dan Issel: Scored over 27,000 points between the ABA and the NBA. Seven time All-Star

Louie Dampier: Twelve year pro, nine of the seasons in the ABA. All-time leading scorer in ABA history

Cliff Hagan: Five-time NBA All-Star selection and a player/coach in the ABA

Tayshaun Prince: Four-time All-NBA Defensive selection, and gold medal winner with the 2008 U.S. Olympic team

Frank Ramsey: Sixth man for the Boston Celtics dynasty, won seven NBA titles

---

After the 2013–14 season, two Cats left for the NBA after one season of college ball—and they ended up on bitter professional rivals. Julius Randle (30) was drafted by the Los Angeles Lakers, while James Young (1) was drafted by the Boston Celtics. (Tim Sofranko)

While critics of the program have argued that the "one and done" trend of modern college basketball deprives players of long-lasting roots with their colleges, or the college fans of really getting to know the players, it's clear that the people advancing those arguments don't follow Kentucky. Kentucky fans equally love and celebrate the full spectrum, from four-year players like Toronto's Chuck Hayes to Oklahoma City's Enes Kanter, who never actually played a minute for UK. Once a Wildcat, always a Wildcat.

If traveling several hours and spending large amounts of money is impractical, there is a much cheaper and easier way to follow your favorite NBA Cats—social media. Twitter is probably the most common denominator for checking of UK legends, and while Twitter profiles and handles change constantly, a few of the most notable ones are listed below. Many of the former Wildcats are just as Internet-addicted as your typical UK fan, and enjoy interacting with fans in real time on the World Wide Web.

Anthony Davis: @AntDavis23

John Wall: @JohnWall

DeMarcus Cousins: @Boogiecousins

Patrick Patterson: @pdpatt

Rajon Rondo: @RajonRondo

Michael Kidd-Gilchrist: @MKG14

Julius Randle: @J30_Randle

Willie Cauley-Stein: @THEwillieCS15

Various: @ExCats (A *Lexington Herald-Leader* account to follow the NBA Cats)

Attend a Basketball Practice in the NCAA Tournament

WHERE: Anywhere the teams play, but for our purposes, we're concentrating on NCAA Tournament sites

WHEN: Only certain times. Watch ukathletics.com or your favorite UK news sites for up-to-the-moment details during the tournament.

HOW TO DO IT: All you have to do is drive there

COST FACTOR: $ Most of the time these things are free. You may have to pay to park.

DIFFICULTY FACTOR: ▮ Great way to see your favorite team

BUCKET RANK: 🗑

HINTS FOR LITTLE WILDCATS/RELUCTANT WILDCATS:
Normally, these are great environments for little Wildcats. There's music and activity everywhere, and if the kiddos tend to get bored then you can just leave whenever you want. At no cost, there's no loss.

• •

Normally, if you want to see a UK basketball practice, you need to know someone to get in. Now, here we're talking about a real practice, one where there's little to no media, held at the Joe Craft Center, led by coach John Calipari and with the actual goal of improving some part of the team.

In all honesty, a normal fan will not get to see this environment. It's behind closed doors. If you're going to see a practice like this, more than likely you know Cal, or maybe one of the assistant coaches, and they've been able to let you in. Of course, you'd better keep quiet—and there's a rule that you cannot report (to anyone) what you see.

So we're not going to talk about that in this space. Luckily, for UK fans, there are several other instances where you can see your Wildcats practice, the most fun being in the "open" practices held for the fans and media in the weeks leading up to NCAA games.

Our recommendation is—if you ever get the chance—to see your Wildcats practice in the final week of the season leading up to the Final Four. In 2015, when Kentucky made the Final Four, we were able to go and watch the open practice, held on the Friday before the Final Four. Thousands of others showed up, too. It was a Big Blue Family.

Obviously, first you have to drive. Indianapolis is close for us, so we took advantage, driving the two hours up to Indy. Open practices are free—but parking is not—so bring some cash so you can park close and walk on in. For ladies, there are also restrictions on bags, so get on the NCAA website and find out what you can and cannot take in. Plan accordingly.

When you find a parking space, make sure to take some pictures—you're there. You're at the Final Four! When you walk in, you'll receive a ticket (remember—it's all free) and you'll go through security before entering the stadium. Get there early, because you can sit wherever you want. Make your way down as close to the court as you can.

Now with these practices, coach John Calipari doesn't like to do a lot of what we would call real practicing—a lot of the normal drills and such are forsaken for more of a fan-friendly three-point shooting and dunking experience. But in the Final Four Cal does things a bit differently, and in 2015 he gave fans a bit of a look behind the curtain as to how real practices are conducted.

First, all of the players were introduced and cheered for (unless you were one of the few odd Indiana fans who came to Lucas Oil Stadium. Those sad sacks. I felt like telling them, "Yeah, this is what the Final Four looks like. And it's the only way you'll ever see it."). Then they got down to business: a 40–50 minute run-through of some of the staples of their true practices.

It starts with individual instruction for the big men. This could involve the assistant coaches (holding huge foam pads to increase their height) playing defense against the centers and forwards as they rise up and take baby hook shots. By the way, it seems like the big men never miss.

On the other end of the court, the guards (and sometimes the small forwards) will be working on the lost art of basketball: the midrange jumper. They will be passed the ball, they will pump fake, take a step or two inside the three-point arc, and take the shot. Most of the time it seems like they go through the net.

Other players may be shooting free throws. Again, the guards seem to never miss. The big men? It's a little tougher for them.

Then we go to the most fascinating drill you'll get to see. Three players at a time will run down the court—no dribbles, just passing—on a fast break. The amount of distance these long players are able to cover is amazing. A player will catch the ball coming through the hoop after a made shot and immediately outlet to a guard, who will catch, look up, and hit a teammate in stride as he drives in for a layup.

A player is waiting for the ball to come through the hoop, and he will outlet a pass and the drill starts all over again. It's like a ballet, it's so graceful.

The ball will not touch the floor, and the players are encouraged to hit a certain number of layups in a certain amount of time, so it all happens very fast.

That alone is worth the price (again—free) of admission.

Afterward, you'll see some more big men shooting free throws and you'll see shooting guards practicing feeding the post, then taking a pass back out to shoot a three. On the day that I saw practice, Devin Booker looked like he never missed a shot. Obviously, the guy can shoot. It was just beautiful to watch the guy shoot the rock.

After about 40 minutes, the players each came out and waved to the crowd, and they were given a rousing send-off. And, after some Big Blue cheering by the crowd, we exited.

But it wasn't the end of the day—not by a long shot. This is why you want to do this at the Final Four.

You've got to see the Final Four Fan Fest. After your team has had its open practice, go to the city's convention center, where you'll be able to find the festival. Held at many of the championship sites over the years (like the Super Bowl, All-Star Games, etc.) the Fan Fest is a way to bring families into the event with games, trivia, autograph signings and more.

The Final Four Fan Fest may be the best of them all. You'll want to check it out. It's $10 to enter ($5 for students) and once you get in (there will be long lines as they herd people through the doors) you'll be on sensory overload. Everywhere, there are physical challenges for little ones (shooting drills, games, etc.), meet-and-greets with former college greats and current broadcasting celebrities, food and drinks, merchandise for sale, and even a live rock band. Plus, you can get your picture taken with the NCAA championship trophy and have the kids climb an official ladder to cut down some championship nets. The picture opportunities alone are worth it.

In 2015, you could meet celebrities such as former UK stars Jamal Mashburn and Antoine Walker, former Duke stars Jay Williams and Christian Laettner, former Michigan State stars Morris Peterson and Steve Smith, West Virginia Coach Bob Huggins, and Texas Tech Coach Tubby Smith.

You can easily spend a few hours looking around and meeting people. Fans of all teams will be entertained.

After playing your way through the Fan Fest you can then look for another great part about Final Four weekend: the live music. In past years, free concerts have been performed by artists such as Bruce Springsteen, Fun., and Zac Brown Band.

Again: Free.

We saw Cold War Kids, Weezer, and Imagine Dragons.

Not bad.

—Ryan

Meet Up with UK Fans Across the Country

No matter where you are, you're never far away from the Big Blue Nation. After all, there's a reason we call it that, right? Big Blue *Nation*.

It's because no matter where you are, it always seems that you can find Big Blue Brethren around you. If you are, for some ungodly reason, outside of the wonderful commonwealth of Kentucky when a huge basketball game is about to be played, fear not.

We've got you covered. Here's a very short (and incomplete) list of some of the more popular places to visit when you're out of town. These places make you feel right at home—no matter who's winning or losing. When you're in these towns, you're always going to find the Big Blue Nation at these hangouts:

Atlanta, Georgia: Stout Irish Pub, 56 E. Andrews Drive NW, No. 16, Stoutirishpub.com

Alpharetta, Georgia: TJ's Sports Bar & Grill, 2880 Holcomb Bridge Road, Tjssportsbar.com

"Fans in Catlanta frequent both establishments," Jeffrey Neil Burch, then-president of the Greater Atlanta alumni chapter, told the *Herald-Leader* in 2012. "The Stout Irish Pub's upstairs is decorated with Wildcat banners and is a favorite among younger alumni….TJ's has its share of pennants and banners, and offers fans discounts during the games."

Austin, Texas: Uncle Billy's Brewery & Smokehouse, 1530 Barton Springs Road, www.unclebillysaustin.com

Many a UK fan enjoyed the 2014 Final Four watching party at this smokin' joint.

Charlotte, North Carolina: IceHouse, 2100 South Boulevard, Icehousesouthend.com

Chicago, Illinois: The Pony, 1638 W. Belmont Avenue, Theponychicago.com/alumni

This legendary UK fan outpost is famous for making T-shirts every season for Kentucky fans. Recent shirts claimed the Pony as the wearer's "New Kentucky Home." Try the Big Blue, a vodka drink with grape juice, blue Curacao, and Sprite. Then have seven more to commemorate UK's eight national titles. Just kidding. One is probably enough.

Columbus, Ohio: Chubby's, 1846 Hard Road, www.facebook.com/chubbyssportsbarandgrillonhard

Denver, Colorado: College Inn, 4400 E. Eighth Avenue, Collegeinndenver.com

Hilton Head, South Carolina: Steamer Seafood, 1 N. Forest Beach Drive, No. 28, Coligny Plaza, Steamerseafood.com

"Kentucky native Dale Augenstein's restaurant features plenty of UK memorabilia and often hires Kentucky college students in the summers," *Herald-Leader* reader Joe Nell Barnett told the newspaper. A second location is planned for Bowling Green, Kentucky.

New Orleans, Louisiana: Huck Finn's Cafe, 135 Decatur Street, www.huckfinnscafe.com

For the 2012 Final Four, the place to be was Huck Finn's, as the restaurant even gave out free Final Four glasses with the purchase of drinks.

New York City: Jack Demsey's, 36 W. 33rd Street, Jackdemseys. com or NYCukalumni.com

Possibly the most famous outside-the-state spot for game-watching UK fans, this is the home of the New York chapter of the UK Alumni Association. It's easy to tell their allegiance—there's a UK flag flying under the sign outside. It's like a beacon, welcoming us home.

New York-native players like Ramel Bradley have been known to drop by from time to time to watch games. Here, a UK fan feels truly at home.

San Francisco, California: Zeke's Sports Bar & Grill, 600 Third Street, www.facebook.com/zekesbar

Herald-Leader reader Ashley Mason says as many as 40 fans will gather here for big basketball games, and that it all started back in 1994, when a group watched UK come back from 31 points down in the second half to beat LSU.

Tampa, Florida: Beef O'Brady's, 2819 S. MacDill Avenue, Uktampabay.com

You can also see a UK flag flying here on game day, as the restaurant serves as the game-watching home of Tampa Bay's UK alumni chapter. Look for the specials on Maker's Mark.

Washington D.C.: Grevey's, 8130 Arlington Boulevard, Falls Church, VA, Greveys.com

This is the place for UK fans in the D.C. area. Want Cats jerseys on the walls? You got it. Want memorabilia inside, like old programs and photos? Check. How about a UK legend running the show, stopping to gab with fans about his career? Kevin Grevey can provide it all at his restaurant.

Located in the D.C. suburbs, the place is owned by former UK standout Kevin Grevey, who also played for (and won a world championship with) the Washington Bullets in the NBA.

EXTRA POINTS

And for More Options...

Like we said, this is a very incomplete list, as we wanted to highlight some of the more famous places across the country for UK fans to gather. But if there are other places you find yourself visiting, and you'd like to inquire about viewing parties or the like, contact the UK Alumni Association. They can help direct you to a local chapter.

UK Alumni Association
King Alumni House
400 Rose Street
Lexington, KY, 40506-0119
Phone 859-257-8905 or 1-800-269-ALUM (2586)
Email ukalumni@uky.edu

The only rule? Don't ask him about losing the 1975 national championship to John Wooden and UCLA. It still eats away at him. He'd much rather talk about 1978, when he won his title in Washington, and UK won the national championship over Duke.

"That was a good year, 1978," Grevey says, laughing. "Even now, when I see things with a '78' on it, I buy them."

West Palm Beach, Florida: Palm Beach Ale House, 2161 Palm Beach Lakes Boulevard, Palmbeachalehouse.com.

For those looking for love (admittedly, probably in all the wrong places), don't forget **BBNmeetup.com**, an online dating site for Kentucky fans. The creation of the site in 2015 was big news. The creators of the site maintain that "being a Kentucky sports fan is not just an interest but a way of life." While that is true enough, the jury is still out as to whether Cat fan online romance is reality or fantasy.

· ·

Travel the World with the Cats

Whether it's soaking up the sun on a tropical beach or touring the historic ruins of Rome, there's no vacation like a Big Blue vacation. And for a thief's ransom, you and your loved ones can enjoy the vacation of pretty much everyone's dreams.

No more than once every four years, the Wildcats are allowed by NCAA rules to engage in a foreign tour and play basketball against non-American teams. Before John Calipari's hiring in 2009, the most recent foreign tour had been in 1995, when UK played a series of exhibition games in Italy against local opponents. That trip was somewhat wild. UK guard Cameron Mills suffered an injury, which caused him to miss out on much of the basketball. Coach Pitino was ejected from a loss against Montecatini, prompting bystanders to wonder whether Pitino's Italian or the official's English had been sufficient to bring about the ejection. On the whole, though, UK went 4–1, and Pitino met the Pope, prompting the Coach to joke that he had kissed the papal ring, and the Pope offered to do likewise, before noticing that Pitino didn't yet have a (championship) ring. He would win one soon enough, in large part due to the chemistry created on the Italian trip.

A decade and a half later, John Calipari recognized that extra games and extra practices gave his young UK teams a better chance to bond together, and so a 2010 trip to Canada was organized. While Windsor provides a few delights, Calipari and UK determined that the next trip should be a little more exotic.

Enter the Bahamas. UK played a week's worth of games in a small gymnasium at Nassau, and allowed fans to get their first glimpse of Devin Booker, Karl-Anthony Towns, and Tyler Ulis. Trey Lyles was recovering from an injury, and like the Big Blue Nation, had to console himself with gorgeous scenery. Kentucky went 5–1 on the trip, playing without not only Lyles, but also Willie Cauley-Stein, who was also on the mend from an injury. The team grew in closeness, and the fan base… well, they partied, hit the beaches, and generally lived the high life.

Kentucky's international travel wasn't always this glamorous. In 1951, Adolph Rupp took his NCAA champions on a tour of Puerto Rico. He wrote UK broadcaster Claude Sullivan a postcard, explaining that the team was playing outdoor games on dirt courts, but were "living like kings." Rupp's successor, Joe B. Hall, was excited by the growing international flavor of basketball, and began a relationship with Japan. Many Japanese coaches would spend their summers visiting the United States, and soaking up knowledge at Coach Hall's camps. In return, the UK coach brought teams to Japan in 1978, 1982, and 1986. The 1982 squad also played a game each in Taipei and Hong Kong. Coach Hall's Wildcats had some close calls against foreign national teams, but ultimately went undefeated on the trips.

In the modern era, UK's cultural exchange goes beyond basketball. While in the Bahamas, during a rare moment off, the UK players, rather than hit the beach, participated in a Samaritan's Feet charity event. The Wildcats washed the feet of local Bahamian children, and put them in new socks and shoes. At one point, Karl-Anthony Towns had cleaned a boy's feet, and realized he was out of socks. Towns slipped off his own shoes, and then his socks, and put his socks on the boy's feet. As Towns wears a size 20 shoe, the sock was rolled up to near the boy's knee. It wasn't a buzzer beater or a slam dunk, but Towns made a more significant contribution that day.

While a trip with the Wildcats may not net you Karl-Anthony Towns' socks, there's no question that it offers relatively personal moments with fellow fans and Wildcats. Great sites, a fun travel experience, and some world-class basketball. What's not to love?

Watch UKAthletics.com for information regarding future foreign trips.

Chapter 5

Your Own UK Universe

From Lexington to across Kentucky to the rest of the nation to the world. Surely, you're thinking, we're out of space. No way. This chapter is dedicated to building your own UK universe—right where you are. If you can't get out and travel, then we've still got plenty of ideas to occupy you. Time to build your own UK man (or woman) cave, read up on UK history, even listen to some UK-related music. And wherever you may be, you can always argue about your own all-time UK basketball dream team, and celebrate UK's latest triumphs.

Build Your (Wo)Man Cave. Or Room. Or Whatever.

I had a man cave once. It was glorious.

My wife and I had recently moved, and the new house had a partially finished basement. I quickly bought a big-screen television and set about making the room my own man cave.

It took about four guys to help move in that giant television. The guy who loaned me the van to haul it over told me, "Ryan, you're going to watch UK win a national championship on that TV." Two years later he looked like a prophet, because I watched UK win their eighth national championship on that TV.

Inside the room there were shelves with bobbleheads and sports toys. There was autographed memorabilia. There were two couches and plenty of wall space for framed jerseys, pennants, or flags.

And at one point, I had it all. I had old newspapers that I had saved from big wins. There was Patrick Sparks hitting three free throws in the final seconds to beat Louisville. There was Anthony Davis celebrating that national championship.

There were small autographed portraits of former UK stars like Jodie Meeks, Jeff Sheppard, and Rex Chapman. There were framed selfies of me with Ashley Judd, Tubby Smith, and John Calipari. There were signed basketball cards from Rajon Rondo, Dan Issel, and Tony Delk. There were replica championship rings from 1996 and 2012. There were framed Sports Illustrated covers from 1996, 1998, and 2012. There were posters from various Big Blue Madness giveaways, a Calipari-signed basketball commemorating the team's 2000th win, two other signed balls—one with the signatures of the 2012 starting five, another with the entire 1978 championship team on it—and there was even a piece of the New Orleans floor from the 2012 championship.

It was all displayed tastefully of course, even if everybody didn't necessarily think so.

"What's that rag doing tacked to the wall?" one family member asked.

Of course, I explained it was the 1992 Rally Rag given out to fans at the Unforgettables' Senior Night.

"Who were the Unforgettables?" the family member asked.

What could I say? It was too much to explain.

On the bookshelf, there were countless UK-related books by authors such as Russell Rice, Cawood Ledford, Tom Leach, Rick Pitino, Dick Vitale, John Calipari, John Feinstein, and David Halberstam. On the wall was a pennant commemorating the Wildcats' eight championships. On top of the television was a UK gnome (a gift from my niece), along with other knickknacks like commemorative shot glasses and mugs. There was some UK pasta (little basketballs) and some UK hot sauce. There were three very lovely Maker's Mark bottles featuring those same Unforgettables, Calipari, and Tim Couch.

Tacked on walls were detailed figurines of former Kentucky players now in the pros: Rajon Rondo, Anthony Davis, John Wall, and Tayshaun Prince.

And in really nice frames were autographed pictures of Anthony Davis dunking on Louisville and a Final Four poster. I had waited in long lines to get some of the items signed. I spent a bit of money to hang them up. It was, if I can be so candid, an awesome setup.

But even then, I think I knew it wouldn't last.

If there was ever a moment when a child—my own or someone else's—would come downstairs, there was always a chance something would get broken. Or ruined. I could see the writing on the wall—even though there wasn't physically much room left on the walls because of all the memorabilia.

I got it. The man room was going to quickly become the kid room.

And so, over a Christmas break, I condensed some of the collection, and moved the rest of it up to the guest room. I figured if I could make it tasteful, my wife would approve.

But how does one do that? First, it comes down to the framing.

You don't just want to tack some stuff up on a wall. It doesn't look good, and you never want to put a hole in your stuff. So get it professionally framed and matted. Make it look good. That increases how much it's worth.

Of course, you want to save and showcase your autographed memorabilia. Cards and pictures can go in albums and be put on the Internet. And those can go on bookshelves. Put your best stuff out there—and really get it professionally framed—and people will love it.

So I went about displaying the memorabilia in a much smaller space. I'd like to think I still have a pretty good collection. People love to come over and look at the stuff. Of course, for me, it's like stepping back in time. A lot of these memories occurred with family members and friends. I needed a place to keep some of this stuff, so it's good that I sort of got to keep my man room. It's not a cave anymore, and it's got a much smaller television inside it, but it's just fine.

Now, my daughter's toys occupy the former man cave. She loves watching SpongeBob on the giant television.

And I'm still getting more stuff all the time.

These days, I have to really pick and choose what I feature.

—Ryan

Wildcat Bookshelf

I t's common technique for writers or broadcasters to term UK athletics as one of the most storied programs in NCAA competition. Where it gets extra fun is tracking down and reading some of those stories. Because there's no offseason in books, here are a few of the numerous UK-related books that Wildcat fans may enjoy.

UK History

Former UK Sports Information Director Russell Rice wasn't the first to write about UK, but his histories of Wildcat basketball (*Kentucky's Big Blue Machine*) and football (*The Wildcats*) are essential starting places for those who like to know the old stories. Rice has penned a few modern books, including a nice biography of Adolph Rupp in the 1990s.

Father-son duo Bert and Steve Nelli combined for a nice coffee-table history, *The Winning Tradition*, which provides history and some nice photography. Gregory Kent Stanley's *Before Big Blue* chronicles UK sports before 1940, which is an often ignored segment of UK history. For a UK basketball overview, Tom Wallace's *University of Kentucky Basketball Encyclopedia* is a classic.

Biographies

Most major UK figures of recent years have penned autobiographies covering their Wildcat years. The books are usually thin and quick to read, but always provide some insight into some of UK's best. A few of those UK stars/authors include Tim Couch, Richie Farmer, Jeff Sheppard, Cameron Mills, and Derek Anderson.

UK coaches are inevitably the subject of books, whether self-penned or otherwise. A multitude of Rupp biographies circulate, and Joe B. Hall was the subject of a book from Russell Rice. Rick Pitino's

Full-Court Pressure documents the inside story of the 1992 Wildcat season, while John Calipari's recent *Players First* included the 2012 UK title march. Wildcat football coaches are generally at less of a premium, but the multitude of books on Bear Bryant sometimes discuss his Lexington days, and Wildcat head man Rich Brooks was the subject of *Rich Tradition*, a fun book from Tom Leach in 2009 that remembered the glory days of his tenure in Lexington.

Profiles in Catdom

Another common approach is profiling memorable Cats. Jamie Vaught wrote no fewer than four books providing profiles of outstanding Wildcats, and while all four are now out of print, each is a very pleasant read. We can't be unbiased about Ryan Clark's *Game of My Life: Kentucky Wildcats*, but it tells the story of 30 Wildcats and their greatest games. We can be equally positive about Doug Brunk's *Wildcat Memories*, which similarly profiles legendary UK players and discusses mentors who helped them through their UK days.

Controversy

For those who want to explore the darker corners of UK history, Shannon Ragland's *Thin Thirty* is a fascinating recounting of UK football coach Charlie Bradshaw's 1962 squad—and the failures that kept Bradshaw and UK from football glory. In a more recent vein, disgruntled former UK football assistant coach Tony Franklin's book *Fourth Down and Life to Go* contains tons of great stories of the Hal Mumme UK football era. Franklin's writing can be very hit-and-miss, but the content makes sure that Franklin is a better author than we are football coaches. Betty Coles' *Kentucky's Domain of Power, Greed, and Corruption* is as cheery as the title suggests, but is interesting, if sometimes a bit misguided.

Miscellanea

A few more books defy category, but deserve mention. Lonnie Wheeler's *Blue Yonder* is a fascinating catch-all look at UK basketball culture. Written in 1998, much of the book holds true today. Our

There are plenty of UK books you need to fill up your library. Coaches, players, even radio broadcasters have written them. And yes—we think you need them all. Start with **The Kentucky Wildcats Fans' Bucket List.** (Ryan Clark)

own humble effort, *100 Things Wildcats Fans Should Know and Do Before They Die*, has started a few arguments and provided a fun overview of UK history. If you want to review the UK–Louisville roundball rivalry, you might check out our *Fightin' Words: Kentucky vs. Louisville.* Joe also collaborated with Alan Sullivan on a biography of UK broadcasting legend Claude Sullivan, *Voice of the Wildcats*, and Ryan worked with Denny Trease on a UK overview, *Tales from the Kentucky*

THE STRANGE CASE OF CARLOS TOOMER

Who: A very obscure player, and possibly a very bizarre poet, but probably just a clue into the depths of Big Blue Craziness.

Why: It's all in the words

Where to Find Him: The real Toomer was last noted to be serving in the Air Force. The poet Toomer has been oddly quiet.

A rose by any other name would be…well, ask UK's quasi basketball poet laureate, Carlos Toomer. First, a couple words of background. Toomer was a lightly recruited guard who was a semicontroversial signee by Rick Pitino in 1990. In two years at UK, he scored 26 points, and then transferred to St. Louis.

Meanwhile, in the underworld of the Internet, in the late 2000s, a random poet surfaced, calling himself Carlos Toomer, and penning a series of poems with some peripheral connection to UK basketball. Now, obvious possibilities hold : a. the poet actually is *the* Carlos Toomer; b. the poet happens to be another person named Carlos Toomer; or c. the poet is not Carlos Toomer at all, but for some reason claims to be.

Option c is by far the leader in the clubhouse, particularly based on the nature of some of the poems. In the interest of not being sued by either a real or fake Carlos Toomer, here is just a brief burst of one poem, titled "Wayne Turner (U of K) 1996–2000": "You are who you are/I am who I am, I'm here if you need me."

It has been almost a decade since the Carlos Toomer poems surfaced, and I'm still not sure what I think. Part of me hopes this really is the Carlos Toomer, writing odd poems. Part of me is impressed with the potential fandom of a mediocre poet who attaches an obscure UK basketball name to his or her poems. In the end, who knows? Google the poems, read them, and ponder. That's good enough for me.

—Joe

Wildcats Locker Room. We don't want to brag on ourselves, but our moms still claim us.

If you're buying for a little Wildcat, Dale Due's *You Are a Kentucky Wildcat* is a must. Born-again Wildcats may appreciate Ed McMinn's *Daily Devotions for Die-Hard Fans: Kentucky Wildcats*. There is even a Joanne and Rick Pitino cookbook, although most Wildcat backers would probably indicate that the recipes are stale by about two decades.

Still Is Still Moving

Former UK women's basketball All-American Valerie Still deserves special mention. Her two volumes on the Underground Railroad, written for young readers, mean that not only is Valerie the leading scorer and rebounder in UK history, but she's also the top author.

· ·

Check Out the Cats in Movies

Come March, the camera always finds its target. It's not the three-point-bombing shooting guard, or the athletic power forward or strong center. It's not even the multimillion-dollar man in the fancy suit. No, year in and year out, the camera finds the lady in a baseball cap and a UK T-shirt. You see, Ashley Judd is kind of a big deal. And if you didn't know that, CBS, ESPN, etc., will make sure that you do.

To her credit, Ashley has been a major UK fan at least since her own days on campus in Lexington. When she made her mark in Hollywood, she didn't change her stripes, famously turning down the offer of a North Carolina jacket on set once, with a rejoinder that she would rather freeze than wear the offending garment. With fame and fortune came the opportunity to befriend the players, get prime seats at the games, and generally act like the superfan that she is.

Ashley is far from alone in her Cat fandom in Hollywood. Here are a few big UK supporters, and some of their finer moments on the big screen:

Ms. Judd: *Kiss the Girls* (1997), *Double Jeopardy* (1999), *Divine Secrets of the Ya-Ya Sisterhood* (2002), the *Divergent* series (2014, 2015).

Josh Hutcherson: Before he starred opposite alleged Lousiville fan Jennifer Lawrence in the *Hunger Games* films, Josh spent his early years in Kentucky before the call of stardom drew him westward. Josh's defining film moments have been the *Hunger Games* series, but he's diverse—he's been a guest on Kentucky Sports Radio and has hosted *Saturday Night Live*.

George Clooney: He's a little more subtle about it, but Clooney is an acknowledged Cat fan. He grew up in Kentucky, and his father, television star Nick Clooney, told us that he played center on a terrifically awful high school team. Nowadays, he's a two-time Academy Award winner and a verifiable star. His highlights include *From Dusk Till Dawn* (1996), *O Brother, Where Art Thou* (2000), and *Ocean's Eleven* (or *Twelve*, or *Thirteen*—with the first film released in 2001).

Steve Zahn: Zahn is from Minnesota, but married a local lady, and has proclaimed his devotion for the Big Blue. His cinematic career has included roles in *Reality Bites* (1994), *That Thing You Do* (1996), and *You've Got Mail* (1998), but his great supporting work in buddy comedy *Saving Silverman* (2001) is perhaps his funniest moment.

Not only are there movies from Wildcat fans, there are movies *with* Wildcats. A few of the highlights:

Travis Ford shows up in 1997's *The Sixth Man* alongside Marlon Wayans, as basketball player Danny O'Grady.

Walter McCarty was one of a bevy of ballplayers in 1998's *He Got Game*, in which he played Mance. McCarty played alongside Syracuse's John Wallace in the film—probably more fun for Walter since his Cats beat Wallace's Orangemen in the 1996 NCAA title game, which was both players' last college game.

Rick Pitino makes a brief cameo as himself in *He Got Game*, and in 1994's *Blue Chips*.

Mark Krebs, a Wildcat walk-on, has pursued acting jobs, and makes appearances in a handful of small, independent films.

More directly, there are movies actually about the phenomenon of Kentucky basketball itself. Here's a thumbnail sketch of a few.

- *Sixth Man* is a 2013 documentary that contemplates the nature of hardcore Big Blue fandom.

- *Red v. Blue* is a 2013 documentary about the UK and U of L rivalry. Lots of great cameos, including—wait for it—coauthor Ryan Clark, holding forth on the rivalry.

- *Blue Dawn* is a 2010 film following John Calipari's first season at UK. It is fascinating mostly for the behind-the-scenes access to the team.

- *Going Big* was a 2012 *SEC Storied* TV movie featuring the life and career of UK big man Sam Bowie. It is typical of ESPN's recent film work, and is very much worth a viewing. Similarly, Wildcats Jamal Mashburn and Antoine Walker were featured in the ESPN film *Broke*.

- *History of Kentucky Basketball* and *100 Years of Kentucky Basketball* were released in 2007 and 2006, respectively, and are historical looks back at the UK program.

In addition, season-highlight films are a fascinating reminder of great UK squads. During the Pitino years, a more-or-less annual season highlight VHS tape was produced. In modern years, these have become a bit more unusual—although the 2012 basketball-season-in-review DVD brought the series back. The videos—old or new—are a chance to see the great plays and players, with highlights usually featuring the current Voice of the Wildcats.

Finally, there is a small network of people who trade DVD copies of old UK broadcasts. There are yet others who post them on YouTube or other video sites. Based on the questionable legality of same, we won't name names or websites, but this stuff is out there—a ton of it actually. For their part, the NCAA will sell "official" DVDs of a handful of great Wildcat games. It's very much the tip of the iceberg of UK games on video, but it is officially available.

· ·

Wildcat Music

In UK terms, no sound is sweeter than what SEC broadcaster Joe Dean used to call "STRIIIING MUSIC!" But the swish of the jump shot aside, there's plenty of UK-related music that is also pretty nice.

UK Fans

Basketball and music are two of the most integral parts of Kentucky's heritage. In light of that fact, and the widespread popularity of the Big Blue, it's hardly surprising that several major musical acts have UK fan ties. Some of those:

- Canadian rapper Drake has such a close friendship with the UK program that he was allowed to participate in the layup lines at Big Blue Madness in 2014. He promptly airballed a three-point try. Guess he should stick with rhyming.

- Country star Miranda Lambert has been seen rocking UK shirts on several occasions.

- Hip-hop/basketball mogul Jay-Z has taken in an occasional game in Rupp Arena. He also took in an NBA game with UK star James Young, although James was caught by courtside photographers apparently eyeing Jay-Z's friend Rihanna. We've all been there, James.

- Country outlaw legend Waylon Jennings was fast friends with UK coach/soon-to-be outlaw Eddie Sutton. Waylon hosted the 1988 UK squad at his home in Nashville before the team played Vanderbilt.

- Country brothers John Michael Montgomery and Eddie Montgomery (of Montgomery Gentry fame) are well known Cat backers.

- He might be (in)famous as a member of the Backstreet Boys, but Kentuckian Kevin Richardson is still an avid UK fan, years after his boyhood. Fellow Backstreet Boy Brian Littrell is a Lexington native, and apparently is also a fan.

UK Players and Coaches

Sometimes the music doesn't come to the Wildcats. Sometimes, the Wildcats come to the music. A few notable instances:

- Of all the musical Wildcats, perhaps the most unlikely suspect is Coach Joe B. Hall. But his 1981 album *Kentucky Calling Me* undoubtedly sold more copies than one would suspect. You haven't heard "The Gambler" or the *Dukes of Hazzard* theme song until you've heard Coach Hall's renditions. Bonus points to the coach for somehow involving other legends like Cawood Ledford and Al McGuire.

- Wildcats star Walter McCarty, on the other hand, was a singing sensation even before his Wildcat days. While sitting out the 1992–93 season, Walter sang the national anthem before a game.

His 2003 album, *Moment for Love,* is a taste of Walter's R&B/soul style. Songs like "Freaky Wit Me" and "Feel Like Lovin' You" might be better for after the little Wildcats have gone to bed. A 2011 album, *Emotionally,* picks up where the first left off.

- Wildcat safety Marcus McClinton was a hard hitter on the football field. When his team needed a little inspiration in making a run to a bowl game in 2006, Marcus's penned an up-tempo anthem, "We Believe," which was played with an accompanying video on the scoreboard before UK home games. The song became a theme song for the '06–'07 Wildcats, who won 16 games, including bowl victories over Clemson and Florida State. As recently as 2010, McClinton was still performing R&B music in the Lexington area.

- UK basketball star Trey Lyles isn't a musician, but his father Tom is. Tom Lyles (aka T. Lyles) penned a song, "BBN," about the UK program. He also has additional releases in a more classical R&B vein, including a smooth-as-silk cover of "If You Don't Know Me By Now." That said, no comment on 1997's *4The Sex of It.*

Online Musical Marvels

For a sampling of some of the legendary UK-related musical moments, type up a few of these moments in the Youtube searchbox:

- UK fan Daniel Solzman made hip-hop history with "Lazy Tuesday," the best (or worst) song possibly ever. I could say more, but let's just say, "We're talking 'bout Kentucky b-basketball."

- Kentucky Sports Radio legend Kentucky Joe's ode to Willie-Cauley Stein is the stuff of legends. Possibly insane legends, but we're not splitting hairs.

- In the "Gone but Not Forgotten" subcategory of the same group, the late, great Oh Napier loved to sing about Kentucky basketball. You'll laugh, you'll cry, you may spit your soft drink out your nose.

In Muhlenberg County, home of the Everly Brothers, residents are equally proud of the UK basketball player who grew up there: Patrick Sparks. In fact, there are a lot of places around the state that produced UK basketball players and famous musicians. (Ryan Clark)

If you'd rather appreciate the sublime than laugh at the hysterical, Kentucky teen Marlana VanHoose's performances of the national anthem are absolutely brilliant. It feels wrong to even list Marlana in the same entry as the above performers, because her performances are nothing short of astounding. VanHoose was born blind, but it only means she hasn't seen the literally thousands of tears that her performances have drawn. She's courageous, she's talented, and she is true Big Blue—which may be the only thing she has in common with the performers listed above.

Hoops and Music Road Trips

In light of Kentucky's twin passions and their intersections, one fun way to experience both is a hoops-and-music road trip. A couple of possibilities:

- The darlin' of Butcher Hollow, Kentucky, Loretta Lynn, is nothing less than full-fledged country music royalty. Her birthplace is now a museum (at Millers Creek Road, Van Lear, Kentucky), and about ten miles away, Wildcat All-American John Pelphrey led Paintsville High School to hardwood glory. It's easy to find a friendly local who remembers one or both. The Breaks Interstate Park is about 60 miles east, and for those who like hiking and nature, it's as unforgettable as the Coal Miner's Daughter or the lanky redhead with the deadly three-point shot.

- Big hits came out of Muhlenberg County, Kentucky, where Don and Phil Everly, better known as the Everly Brothers, grew up. There's a local museum and a monument to the famous duo. Big shots were the trademark of Muhlenberg's other favorite son, UK star Patrick Sparks. Bluegrass legend Bill Monroe grew up in nearby Ohio County, where his former home is now a museum. That's a lot of star power for a small area of central Kentucky (even without including John Prine, who immortalized the area in his song "Paradise").

Here are a few other Kentucky music-and-hoops pairings:

Ashland
UK fame: Larry Conley
Music fame: The Judds and Billy Ray Cyrus (in nearby Flatwoods)

Bowling Green
UK fame: Josh Carrier
Music fame: Nappy Roots, Cage the Elephant, members of the Black Crowes, the Hilltoppers

Covington
UK fame: Dicky Beal
Music fame: Haven Gillespie (wrote "Santa Claus Is Coming to Town")

Hazard
UK fame: Johnny Cox
Music fame: Country stars Patty Loveless and Dwight Yoakam (who were born up the road in Pikeville)

Lexington
UK fame: Jack Givens, Mel Turpin, Cameron Mills, James Lee, Vernon Hatton, Thad Jaracz, Dirk Minniefield
Music fame: Country/pop singer Laura Bell Bundy, banjo player J.D. Crowe, Brian Littrell and Kevin Richardson of the Backstreet Boys, and country singer John Conlee (in nearby Versailles)

Louisville

UK fame: Ralph Beard, Winston Bennett, Derek Anderson, Rajon Rondo, Scott Padgett

Music fame: My Morning Jacket, Tantric, Days of the New, jazz band leader Lionel Hampton, Joan Osborne, Mary Travers (of Peter, Paul, and Mary)

Madisonville

UK fame: Frank Ramsey, Travis Ford

Music fame: Christian musician Steven Curtis Chapman (a bit of a stretch, but it's not too far down the road to Paducah, where Chapman grew up)

Maysville

UK fame: Deron Feldhaus, Darius Miller

Music fame: Rosemary Clooney, and George Clooney (who was raised in nearby Augusta. Remember: he tried to sing "Man of Constant Sorrow" for *O Brother Where Art Thou?* but wasn't good enough)

Owensboro

UK fame: Rex Chapman, Cliff Hagan

Music fame: Johnny Depp was born there (and he has been known to play a few notes when not acting)

Dancin' Fools: From the Big Dance to Learning Big Dances

We know all about the Big Dance at UK. But did you know the Wildcats are pretty famous for actual dancing, too? It's true. We value this so much, we think you should get on YouTube and search for some legendary moves.

It all begins with the John Wall Dance. Let's flash back for a moment. In October 2009, UK basketball fans were eager for good times again. They'd just fired Coach Billy Gillispie for not winning enough games and being borderline abusive to his players. UK had lost in the NIT. Times were not good.

Enter John Calipari, who brought along some pretty nice talent to the program, like DeMarcus Cousins, Eric Bledsoe and—yes—John Wall. Fans' expectations were high, and they were ready to be winners again on the highest level. Wall was just what the Big Blue doctor ordered. He was the star of stars—the coolest player in the land. He was the player everyone else wanted to be.

So leave it to Wall, to steal the spotlight from everyone else at Big Blue Madness. In October 2009, the new version of the Wildcats was presented to the home fans at Rupp Arena. Perched high atop a catwalk, the players appeared in a spotlight in the pitch-dark arena. When their names were called they would make some kind of gesture or do a dance and then walk down to a stage.

Here's the secret: DeMarcus Cousins was originally supposed to do the dance. But he was afraid of heights, and there was no way he could do it. John Wall didn't care. Wall took full advantage of the spotlight, and started dancing, flexing his arm and twisting his wrist to the music.

The crowd of 24,000 went wild.

Immediately, the John Wall Dance became a thing. A hit. Only it wasn't really called the John Wall dance. Turns out, Wall was doing a dance called "the Shizz," made famous by a video by Louisville rapper Kenzo. LaShawn "Sugar Shizz" Talbert performed the dance in the video. When John Wall did it, however, every UK fan from Pikeville to Paducah knew what it was—even if they called it the wrong name.

Everywhere, it seemed popular culture was wrapping its arms around the John Wall Dance. Hip-hop group Troop 41 released "Do the John Wall." Famous UK fan Josh Hopkins—star of TBS' *Cougar Town*—actually did the John Wall Dance in a scene on his show. When Wall was drafted No. 1 by the Washington Wizards, the city made a welcome video for their new point guard, and fellow Washington stars Stephen Strasburg (baseball) and Alex Ovechkin (hockey) both danced the John Wall.

Even Magic Johnson performed the dance when he made an appearance at a UK game in 2010.

Check it out on YouTube. It's the easiest dance you'll ever see.

But there are other examples of Big Blue dancing that need to be investigated. UK Hoops coach Matthew Mitchell has become a legend in his own right for dancing during Big Blue Madness. In fact, it may be the most-asked question leading up to every performance: What will Matthew Mitchell do this year?

There was James Brown one year. Another time it was Bruno Mars (where Mitchell actually *sang*, too). Still other performances were MC Hammer and Michael Jackson. And of course he performed the John Wall Dance, too.

It all started in 2009, when an assistant coach reportedly told Mitchell that if he sang and danced during Big Blue Madness he would get a high-profile recruit that he desperately wanted.

So the coach did just that.

It didn't work. But Mitchell immediately raised the profile of himself and his UK Hoops squad in the process. Mitchell—a natural performer and veteran of a country-music band in the past—has no problem getting up in front of 24,000 people to sing and dance. He's actually very talented.

And his team—along with his fans—love him for it.

"I didn't think anything about the fans," Mitchell said in an interview with ESPN, "but I thought recruits would like it. I was surprised by the reaction from our fans."

Now every year he strives to do something different—and everyone loves to see what is coming next.

Of course there are other dancers we must point out. There were the cloggers at Big Blue Madness. The Boogie Guy. The UK Dance Team. And then there's the kid who gained notoriety through YouTube when he started dancing to Pharell's "Happy" when it started playing during the 2015 KHSAA High School Sweet Sixteen in Rupp Arena.

Peyton Henderson, an 11-year-old student at Royal Spring Middle School in Georgetown, heard the song during halftime of a game. He got up from his seat and started doing his thing, "as the solemn-faced kid pulls off a series of intricately choreographed moves, moving up and down the steps and ultimately shimmying to his knees," the *Lexington Herald-Leader* reported.

Of course, like everything now, it was captured on video. Now the kid is famous, booking spots on *The Late Late Show* and openly campaigning for an interview with Ellen DeGeneres.

"I just heard the song and I just wanted to dance," he told the newspaper.

Now we just want you to see it. It'll make your day.

· ·

Fashion Sense: Collect and Remember UK's Many Uniforms

Long before Oregon was wearing a different uniform for each football game, and before the Fab Five wore their shorts at their ankles, and way before Under Armour was doing God-knows-what with Maryland's logo, Kentucky was the center of the athletic apparel universe.

Of course, it made sense—their coach was an Armani-wearing New Yorker who styled and profiled up and down the sidelines.

But even before Rick Pitino came to UK, the Wildcats were known for their Converse allegiance. Fans would dream of being Kyle Macy or Goose Givens and they would wear their Converse shoes and simple jerseys accordingly. Then, when Eddie Sutton became coach in the mid-80s, and Rex Chapman committed to the Wildcats, UK became a school ripe to sport the new shoes of the day—those from Nike, which just happened to feature a new superstar named Michael Jordan.

Things didn't change much. But when Pitino became coach in 1989, the shoes and uniforms were switched back to Converse. They were simple, with *Kentucky* spread across the front, the players' names on the back. On the (short) shorts, there was a *UK* on the side. The uniforms and shoes were royal blue and white.

More change, however, was on the way.

Converse used UK like a guinea pig, changing the uniforms (especially the shorts) almost annually. One year, there was a wave across the shorts, and it said *Wildcats* on one leg. Another year there was a junglelike, Zubaz quality. Still another year featured spikes on them—and fans ate up all of these creations, while some rivals snickered.

Still, UK was always a part of the conversation. And nothing got people talking like 1996, when UK had a great team and debuted the "denim" look.

In the middle of the season, fans were excited because UK had lost just one game (to John Calipari's No. 1–ranked UMass squad) and were on the road to winning a national championship. Converse, of course, had planned during the middle of the year to debut new uniforms. It all added up to a perfect storm.

The uniforms were denim in color, from the jerseys to the shoes. It was definitely different. Some fans complained because the blue looked more like North Carolina blue than the royal blue to which UK fans were accustomed. Still, fans everywhere wanted to look like their team. They bought up the jerseys.

But they didn't have a long shelf life. After the world watched UK win the national title over Syracuse in 1996 (wearing the jerseys to get past UMass and Calipari in the national semifinals) they were never seen again. Even a recent search on eBay could not turn up any mention of them.

When Tubby Smith replaced Pitino in 1997, UK signed with Nike. It only made sense two of the biggest basketball brands in the nation should team up with one another. So Nike outfitted UK with subtle uniforms, much like the throwbacks they used to wear. The shoes were simple, but powerful, because with the increasing popularity of AAU basketball, Nike's Swoosh meant something.

It meant the best.

And as Kentucky kept surging in basketball, the program began experimenting again with new uniforms. This time, Nike wanted to push the limit a bit. It used Oregon as its test case for football, again providing different uniforms for the Ducks' gridiron squad for every game.

To a much lesser extent, Nike used Kentucky basketball (and a few other schools, like Texas and Duke) for the same purpose. In the last few years, Kentucky has experimented with black uniforms, platinum uniforms, checkerboard patterns, and unis with a few interesting twists. LeBron James has sent along some special updates on more than one occasion.

And as a tribute to fallen equipment manager Bill Keightley, the Wildcats even spent a game with a black *K* in *Kentucky* on the jersey front, and the name 'Keightley' on the back. Other Nike details involved a design that utilized ideas from the silks of Secretariat, the greatest thoroughbred in the history of racing. Still another depicted scenes of the UK campus.

The 2014–15 season began with a team trip to the Bahamas, and again, Nike decided to change up the look of UK's uniforms. This time, Nike decided to take off the long *Kentucky* across the front and replace it with the large, interlocking UK logo. Some fans were disgusted by the look.

What they fail to realize is that most of what Kentucky and Nike decide to do with the uniforms is a direct result of what current kids (meaning recruits) think is cool. If the recruits like it, it is believed that will be yet another reason for them to commit to play at Kentucky. While some fans or alumni may cringe at the thought of a black Kentucky uniform, or not using the full Kentucky name on the jersey, it seems to be a moot point if it helps bring in talent.

You never know exactly what UK will do next with its uniforms, but as long as they are the trendsetters (and the kids think it's cool), no one will have a huge problem with it.

So, what to do if you want to collect some of these relics?

Ask around. Check your local news sites for memorabilia shows. Look online at eBay and Craigslist.

Nike will sometimes sell throwback versions of certain uniforms.

But for the pure bargain hunter, digging deep is the best way to fly. Sure, you can hunt for months and pay $100 for a pair of the famous icicle shorts on eBay. Or you can find them in a Goodwill store in Louisville for a couple of dollars. You tell us what sounds like more fun.

For that matter, ask your aunts and uncles. Ask your grandfather. This seems to be one of the few ways to put your collection together.

Listen to One of Claude Sullivan's Classic UK Broadcasts

WHERE: UK Library, Special Collections, available online at the Kentucky Digital Library

WHEN: 365 days a year

HOW TO DO IT: Visit http://kdl.kyvl.org/catalog/xt754746qt9q/ guide. Click the "browse" link near the game or interview of your choice.

COST FACTOR: Free with internet access

DIFFICULTY FACTOR: 🗑 Only downside is relative difficulty in moving forward or backward in each recording.

BUCKET RANK: 🗑 🗑 🗑

HINTS FOR LITTLE WILDCATS/RELUCTANT WILDCATS:
There are video/audio sync clips of Sullivan's broadcast of Bear Bryant's final UK game in 1953 vs. Tennessee as well as of the 1958 NCAA title game. (Check YouTube!) Some folks will enjoy the audio more with video—although the fragmentary video results in heavily edited audio. For those who appreciate baseball, Sullivan's Cincinnati Reds broadcasts are enjoyable. History fanatics will enjoy his broadcasts from behind the Iron Curtain in the late '50s.

Unfortunately, there is no Big Blue Time Machine. The next best thing is the Claude Sullivan audio recording archives at UK. Sullivan was a Voice of the Wildcats—indeed, based on his preeminence across the state and area, many considered him *the* Voice of the Wildcats—from 1946 to 1967, when he passed away at age 42 due to cancer.

During Sullivan's era, UK broadcasting was not unified under a single network as today. Multiple stations carried multiple broadcasts of Wildcat action, which meant that Sullivan was a peer, contemporary, and competitor with other broadcasters such as Cawood Ledford, Dee Huddleston, and J.B. Faulconer. Claude Sullivan began the Standard Oil Network, which carried his broadcasts around the commonwealth and made him famous for his play-by-play talents.

Sullivan began broadcasting UK games during the era of the Fabulous Five. He was so young that two of the players on that historic team were older than he was. However, Claude rapidly earned his stripes and was routinely honored by his peers and contemporaries, as he won nine consecutive awards for Kentucky Sportscaster of the Year from the Kentucky Broadcasters Association.

During his two-decade career, which focused on UK basketball and football, but also included horse racing, Cincinnati Reds baseball, and various features from his around-the-world travels, Claude Sullivan had the

EXTRA POINTS

- Sullivan's younger son, Alan, wrote a biography of his father, *Voice of the Wildcats: Claude Sullivan and the Rise of Modern Sportscasting* with Joe Cox in 2014. The book's foreword was by current Voice of the Wildcats Tom Leach.

- Sullivan's elder son, David, played for the football Wildcats under Coach Charlie Bradshaw, and went on to broadcast sports for ESPN, among other media outlets.

- A clip from the archives (Claude Sullivan's call of Vernon Hatton's buzzer-beating shot just inside halfcourt to extend a 1957 game against Temple) is included in the current montage that begins UK Network basketball broadcasts.

foresight to make or keep numerous recordings. Decades after his untimely death, his family restored and donated many of his tapes, along with boxes of programs, scorecards, and other miscellanea, to the university.

The restored tapes provide a unique look back at Rupp and Bryant's glory days. Complete and partial recordings of games stretch from the days of George Blanda to those of Dicky Lyons on the gridiron, and from Beard and Groza to Riley and Dampier in basketball. Games aside, rare interviews with Rupp and Bryant provide context into the times, and the Big Blue giants who shaped them.

For those who want to remember or those who were too young to have experienced these moments, there are certainly few delights equal to sitting back in a comfortable chair, starting a broadcast, and letting the golden tones of Claude Sullivan carry listeners away to another time and place.

Listen to and Watch the Coaches' Shows on Radio and Television

I remember going out to the local mall in south Louisville. I was so excited. It was raining out, but that didn't dampen my mood. I was going to see the coach of my Big Blue Kentucky Wildcats.

Every so often, the UK coach would take his radio show on the road. Each week, I would tune in to 84 WHAS to listen to his comments. I never really learned very much, but just listening to the coach talk with fans was an enjoyable experience.

Most of the time the show was based in Lexington, at some upscale eatery. But sometimes, and this was one of those times, the coach would come to Louisville, my hometown. Because it was the largest city in the state, because at least 50 percent of the population of that city was Kentucky fans, it made sense. When I heard the coach would be making an appearance I decided I had to go.

My family and I arrived just before the show began. Already, there were hundreds of fans all decked out in their UK garb. I'd truly never seen so many Kentucky fans in one place. Later, I'd be told there were more than 200 present. I'd never even been to a game yet. I was just 12 years old.

Coach Rick Pitino was the man of the hour. As the storm raged outside, my family and I made our way to the second floor, where we could watch all the festivities from above and still hear the show over the loudspeakers. I believe at the time coach Pitino was talking with Ralph Hacker, and the format was such that fans would call in and ask the coach questions. Of course, with a live audience at the mall, there were also plenty of fans there who wanted to ask questions. Those folks formed a little line at a microphone just beside the table where Rick and Ralph were seated.

I could see it all from my vantage point. It was a great place to be. But I'll always remember two legendary questions from that audience—they were ones that would typify every UK fan experience.

First was a man from Shelbyville. He wore blue overalls and an old cap with a Kentucky *K* on it. He stepped up to the microphone and got the nod from Ralph.

"And now we've got a question from the audience," Ralph said. "Please sir, step up and tell us your name and your question."

"Yes, thank you, Ralph," the man said. "Hello, coach, hello, Ralph. Thank you for comin' out tonight. I'm Tom from Shelbyville and I just had one question for Coach Pitiner."

That's the way people from around there said Pitino's name. Pitiner.

"Hi, Tom," Pitino said. "What's your question?"

Tom cleared his throat. "Well, Coach, I just want to thank you for what you done coaching these basketball boys. I think you're doin' a great job."

"Thanks, Tom," Pitino said.

"But I was wonderin'," Tom continued. "We all know the football squad's been strugglin'. We ain't won a bowl game in 10 years. I just wonder if you'd ever considered coaching our football team, too?"

Polite laughter filled the space as Tom sat back down.

Pitino said no, he did not think about coaching the football team. He said he had all the faith in the world in the current coaching staff. He said he was convinced they could handle the job.

After a few more callers, an older woman approached the microphone and introduced herself as Liz. Decked out in a blue sweater, which looked to be handmade, she fit in well.

"Coach, I was also wondering something," she said. "I know he hasn't played here for a while, but how come you never put in Richie Farmer more?"

Coach Pitino seemed flummoxed for a moment, and the crowd giggled. Pitino got this question a lot when Farmer—a local legend from the eastern Kentucky mountains—was not playing the amount of minutes fans thought he should. But never had Pitino gotten the question *after* a player had left the program.

For a moment, Pitino seemed almost speechless. Then he just started to laugh.

"What about Richie?" was always a running joke in the UK radio world. It seemed wherever the UK coach went, he'd be asked about

APPRECIATE THE MARKETING POWERS OF COACH CAL

There's really no one better at this than John Calipari. He's the best at marketing himself and his program—and that means he's the best at being the coach at UK. No one was better made for this job than Calipari.

There's a reason why the guy has a marketing degree. If you ever see him on a big stage (or even listen to him on his radio show), he is always on message, which is essentially that Kentucky is about making their players' dreams come true. It makes him the best recruiter, a job that he handles himself (not every coach does this—but it is no coincidence that the best coaches, like Coach K, tend to). He also continuously thinks out of the box. In Memphis he aligned his program with Justin Timberlake, who just may be the coolest guy in the world. In Cal's first season at Kentucky he made sure to do the same. This time, on a chance meeting with another hip-hop star, he recruited him as a fan—and the Canadian-born Drake is still a UK fan to this day.

Calipari also saw how important it was to resell his program to the many NBA stars who called Lexington home. Under Billy Gillispie, the program cut ties with many of its former stars (famously, Tayshaun Prince had asked to come work out in Lexington over a summer. During Gillispie's reign, he was told he could not. Instead he went to practice at Georgetown College). Calipari would have none of that. He wanted his current players to see the successful NBA guys, so Prince, Nazr Mohammed, and Rajon Rondo would always have a home in Lexington.

Calipari also never misses a chance to be seen at cool places (big NBA games, boxing matches, the ESPY Awards, etc.) and he never misses a chance to align his program with interesting people. Flip back and check out the "See the Stars" section in the "Ultimate UK Game Day Experience," if you've forgotten.

Clearly, UK games are the cool place to be, and Coach Calipari has made it that way. But of course, you have to put out an entertaining product as well. People have to *want* to be there, and we have to give Calipari the credit for that, too. The numbers speak for themselves: In six years at UK, his record is 190–38, and the Wildcats have been to four Final Fours, finished national runner-up in 2014, and won the championship in 2012. His teams have won three SEC regular season titles and three SEC tournament titles. No other coach has matched his record for Final Four production in that number of years except for John Wooden and Mike Krzyzewski.

It all added up to John Calipari being inducted into the Naismith Basketball Hall of Fame in 2015. On his career at UK alone he would warrant induction, but when you count more than 600 total wins, two other trips to the Final Four, and an NIT championship in 2002 (plus being named Naismith Coach of the Year three times), he was a shoo-in.

Simply, he's the best. All you have to do is listen—or watch him—to know that.

Farmer's playing time. But Liz took it to a new level. It was just the kind of thing you could expect from a UK fan at a radio appearance.

That's why we suggest you always listen to the coaches' call-in radio shows and watch the weekly (or semiweekly) coaches' television programs. To paraphrase Forrest Gump, you never know what you're going to get. Or hear. Or see.

Take Matthew Mitchell, coach of the women's program. At any time you may see him singing, playing guitar, or cooking a special dish with his wife in the kitchen. On coach Calipari's show you may see a different side of one of the assistant coaches, or you may learn something new about one of the star players. (In the era of the "one-

and-done" player, this kind of behind-the-scenes look has become increasingly popular with fans because they do not get as long to really know their heroes. Any bit of information helps, so watching the coach's show makes sense).

Tom Leach hosts the weekly radio show with Coach Calipari, and it's always funny to hear Leach ask a question—because rarely does Cal answer the exact query. Calipari instead will break off midanswer to start talking about something he noticed in the game, or to describe something else entirely. It's all about staying on message (something we'll talk more about it in a moment).

Under coaches like Joe B. Hall, Eddie Sutton, and Rick Pitino, the basketball television show, normally referred to by the coach's name ("The Coach Rick Pitino Show") was must-see TV for fans. Even when it seemed like a 30-minute infomercial for something mundane like diagramming the motion offense, the show was still watched.

When Coach Calipari arrived in 2009, he rebranded the show and made it more about the program. Now it's called "This Is Kentucky Basketball" (possibly a play off of ESPN's "This Is SportsCenter"?) and it airs semi-regularly throughout the Commonwealth.

Of course, if you've missed episodes, or you need to catch up on anything else Cal or UK-related, you need to visit Calipari's website at CoachCal.com. Besides team information, you'll find archives of the coach's television show, as well as feature stories and videos about players, former players, and staff. Alongside KentuckySportsRadio.com, CoachCal.com is a solid one-stop shop for all things UK.

—Ryan

Check Out
The Cats' Pause

These days, it's hard to imagine, but there was a time when sports news was hard to come by, when readers had to wait for newspapers to run box scores from previous games to find out what had happened. For Oscar Combs, the time was 1975, and after listening to some out-of-state UK fans complain about the lack of reliable coverage of the team, Combs realized that he was just the man to fix the problem. A longtime journalist in his own right, he put his training to work, and in 1976 he began grinding out a weekly (during basketball and football seasons) newspaper covering all things UK.

And while much of traditional journalism is in a slow decline, *The Cats' Pause* remains viable four decades on. Combs sold his stock in the periodical decades ago, but a talented staff of knowledgeable writers pump out UK coverage year round. The newspaper has gone to more of a magazine look, with color photography becoming more common. Game recaps are still provided, but feature stories and recruiting tidbits keep *TCP* relevant in the modern era.

A few years back, *TCP* went digital as well, and print subscribers can now read their copies online even earlier than the post office can deliver the hard copy. Special editions are put out on a few annual occasions for the digital folks, in the quest to stay ahead of the game. The catspause.com website offers additional information, now in conjunction with 24/7 Sports, one of the top Internet recruiting services. For a small monthly fee, *TCP* columnists and outside experts will keep fans literally up to the second on the most recent news. Some of us (definitely including me) can be counted on to spend National Signing Day for football hitting "refresh" on *TCP*'s website.

At this point, *The Cats' Pause* has lasted almost as long as Adolph Rupp's coaching career. I read it years ago when I was 11, and my wife's grandfather is still reading it today into his 90s. *The Cats' Pause* is a fixture. And it's not going anywhere.

In rural eastern Kentucky, copies of *The Cats' Pause* were hard for a preteen me to find. This is how I ended up browsing Mr. Craft's back issues in 6th-grade math. But one periodical that I could manage to find was Oscar Combs' other great brainchild—the annual *Cats' Pause Basketball Yearbook*. While the price of $5.95 seemed gigantic at the time, so did the several hundred pages of preseason basketball info—rosters and forecasts for all SEC and Kentucky teams, lengthy sections on high school and recruiting, and more information about UK players and coaches than could be found anywhere else.

The yearbook began in 1979, and after years of collecting, I managed to acquire the full catalog. The first yearbook clocked in at a meager 36 pages, but the most recent dozen or so measure up at around 400. In 2007, the yearbook went to full-book, full-color graphics. Somewhere around the mid-1990s, it became a Christmas tradition for my mom to send me the yearbook. Somewhere around the late 2000s, I got tired of waiting for Christmas, and began my own tradition of buying it early.

If people otherwise don't realize that I'm a lunatic Kentucky fan, I show them my shelves of *Cats' Pause* yearbooks. For those who are of equal devotion, it impresses them as much as a fancy sports car in the garage would. For the rest of the world, they start to question my sanity. But that's ok. That 1980 article on Joe B. Hall's farm is pretty impressive stuff, if I do say so myself.

—Joe

Follow the Year-Round UK Sport: Recruiting

Once upon a time, recruiting was a topic for college coaches— *only* college coaches. Oh sure, there were a few "insiders" who published newsletters breathlessly extolling the virtues of high school kids nobody had ever heard of; but for most fans, recruiting news came a couple of times per year, when the schools released lists of signees and everyone wondered about these players.

These days, certainly in SEC country, there are three major sports seasons: football, basketball, and recruiting. Evaluation is neverending and with teenagers tweeting out their likes, dislikes, thoughts, attitudes, crushes, and ideas, it is literally impossible to get away from recruiting. So what changed, and what does it mean for Cat fans?

First, the evaluation process changed. Once upon a time, talent scouts roamed the edges and peripheries of the backwoods, seeking out great players by word of mouth. Nowadays, between AAU and summer leagues and team camps, coaches have accumulated the vast majority of major prospects in a few locations, and quickly and efficient set about sorting out the best from the merely good.

Second, the coverage is much more thorough and intense. On the Internet, Rivals.com, 247sports.com, and ESPN.com are the three major recruiting services. Each has a large staff of reporters covering specific programs, and each makes it a point of pride to have the newest and best information first.

Third, television and streaming media have changed the game. Many of the best players are on TV or the internet. You're no longer left wondering about a random name from a town you've never heard of.

If you followed Nerlens Noel's recruitment in high school, you may have heard that he wanted to go to Georgetown, or maybe Syracuse. Instead, when it came time to announce his college decision live on ESPN, all he did was turn around—he had the UK logo shaved into the back of his haircut. (Tim Sofranko)

If you're a hardcore fan, you've seen highlight videos, maybe caught a game or two, and figured out the specific strengths and weaknesses of various prospects' games.

Now, as to what it means—it means more football, more basketball, and more entertainment, especially during what used to be the dead periods in a fan's schedule.

But it also means that with a ton of information, the true recruiting fan has to be ready to chuck it all and trust his or her own insight, because even with a wealth of scouting, the talent evaluators aren't perfect.

Here are a few examples from recent years:

- In 2014, the recruiting analysts were right about highly regarded Duke center Jahlil Okafor and UK's Karl-Anthony Towns. That said, two of the three major services ranked Ohio State star D'Angelo Russell behind bumbling Seton Hall guard Isaiah Whitehead, among others. Kansas' Cliff Alexander and Texas' Myles Turner didn't quite live up to the hype.

- On the gridiron, Oregon quarterback Marcus Mariota was a mere three-star recruit, generally ranking behind multiple quarterbacks whom you never heard of—case in point being DaMarcus Smith, who was the backup quarterback at Western Kentucky and is now at North Texas.

- UK football star Alvin "Bud" Dupree was a three-star tight end recruit and was ranked as the 59th best player in Georgia in 2011 by Rivals. Four years later, Dupree is an NFL first-round draft choice. On the other hand, four-star tight end recruit Alex Smith never took a snap for the Wildcats.

Of course, one thing that all talent evaluators can agree on is that John Calipari is a recruiting machine. Given the "one-and-done" nature of elite college basketball, Coach Cal has had a class within the top two of all major services' rankings for each year since his hiring in 2009. For his part, Mark Stoops is upping the wattage on the football side of things. His first three recruiting classes have ranked as high as any in UK football history. Given the nature of great players coming down the pipeline, the third major sport will be alive and well in Kentucky, and Big Blue fans everywhere will all be awaiting the signing and arrival of the next big thing, whoever he may be.

Argue about Your All-Time UK Dream Team

If you hang out long enough around other UK fans, the conversations start happening. Was Jodie Meeks a better shooter than Rex Chapman? Was Travis Ford a better free throw shooter than Kyle Macy? Who jumped higher—Kenny "Sky" Walker or Anthony Davis? But gradually, when we have these conversations, they tend to end up in the same place—who would be on your all-time UK Dream Team? Now, first, there are a few rules.

First, you don't consider older players in the context of matchups in today's game, but in the context of the game they played. So you can't say, "Well, Alex Groza was 6'7" and never took a jump shot. Willie Cauley-Stein would own him." If you look at it that way, he probably would. But Groza was an All-American who was UK's all-time leading scorer when he played. And that's the context in which we consider him.

Second, it's not just about who were the best players—you could take the UK scoring list and jot down the top thirteen names. But you're building a team, and you've got to think of it like a team. So you draw up a starting five, a second five, and three more guys to finish out your imaginary scholarship list and complete your bench. And then you brag about why your team would obliterate all teams. Ever.

The greatest UK point guard ever was an absolute no-brainer until 2010. At that point, John Wall did what he did, and put on a display of how a lead guard can absolutely take over games and consistently will his team to win after win. But at the end of the day, impressive as that is, when Joe made the choice for his offensive leader, he went old school. All Ralph Beard did was lead UK to its first NIT title and first two NCAA titles. And win a gold medal. And be a three-time All-American. And score enough points that he's still 15th in UK history. Yet, he was an even better passer or defender than a scorer. But if you really want to be impressed, watch the old game tapes. He's the guy who is 30 percent faster than everybody else—who looks like, despite being 5'10", he could play today. So he can, on Team Joe. All of this said, Wall was stupefyingly great in all aspects of the game. And if he'd played four years at UK, everybody's brain might have exploded. Joe's got him as the backup, and Team Ryan flip-flops the two, with Wall starting and Beard off the bench.

At shooting guard, the conversation starts and ends with one of the steadiest scorers ever: Tony Delk. Other players were more glamorous, but Delk is fifth on the UK scoring list, and it's because you couldn't stop him. If he was cold from three—which rarely happened—he'd kill you with his pull-up midrange jumper. Or get fouled. He had a

Would the Harrison twins make your all-time UK starting backcourt? Consider this: In two seasons at Kentucky, the pair led their teams to two consecutive Final Fours. They always saved their best for the postseason. (Tim Sofranko)

little running one-hand shot that never seemed to miss in four years. He's also second on UK's steals list, and had the longest arms a 6'1" guy could humanly have. So not only can't you stop him, but he will find a way to stop the opposing shooting guard. For his backup, Joe went with a guy who is the purest shooter ever in Lexington—Louie Dampier. He's 12th on the scoring list, and if the three-pointer had existed, he'd have been higher. If you have doubts on that, consider that he went to the ABA and became pro basketball's first great three-point shooter. You're not going to play zone against a team with Louie. You also wouldn't sag off of Ryan's backup shooting guard. He'd shoot over you, or just drive and dunk right through you. Rex Chapman's game was ahead of its time, and he'd fit right in on an all-time team.

For a small forward, Team Joe drafts the guy who, much like Delk, isn't the most glamorous, but who just got it done. Jack Givens is the third-highest-scoring Wildcat ever. He was a key component on teams that reached two NCAA title games. He was money from midrange—just ask Duke, against whom he scored 41 in the '78 title win. But he was also 12th on the UK rebounding list, and was an 80 percent foul shooter. He wouldn't be the flashiest, but he'd be steady. Kind of like his backup, who was similarly quiet. In four years, Tayshaun Prince never stopped playing hard, but also never stopped making it look easy. Like Delk, he had an incredible wingspan and a great defensive motor. But he also could drive, bomb away, and hit big shots. Good enough for all-time.

Team Joe's power forward is the great Jamal Mashburn—and in fact, he's Team Ryan's small forward. He's the player who did the most to bring UK back from the Eddie Sutton mess. And what didn't he do? He had a nasty streak, and would dunk on opponents with authority. Or he could hang outside and beat them with the jump shot. He also was a man on the backboard, and is still in UK's top 40 in assists! His backup? Well, just the leading scorer in UK history. Dan Issel is one of those guys who might not have looked like a stereotypically great player—but when you looked at the box score, he'd put up 40 and 15 boards. At 6'8", he played an undersized center position, but he could step out on the floor and shoot it. He's good for punch off the bench for Team Joe—or to start alongside Mashburn on Team Ryan.

Team Joe passed on starting a one-year wonder with John Wall, but it didn't happen twice. Anthony Davis was just the best one-year player ever. He did everything in 2012 except sell popcorn, and he probably could've figured out a way to do that better. Davis is Bill Russell–like in his ability to change the game. His counterpart is the great Bill Spivey. Spivey is still the top two-year scorer at UK. He lost his freshman year because of freshman ineligibility and his senior year to injury. But his two seasons were mammoth. He went head-to-head with Kansas's Clyde Lovelette, and owned him. Unfortunately, he was banned from the NBA without any proof of his involvement in the point-shaving scandal. He sued, and the NBA later paid him to settle, but he never got to show the world what he showed at UK. Now, he's getting the chance. Ryan concurred on both spots for his team.

For the last three spots, we could do anything. We could go with Sam Malone, Tod Lanter, and Brian Long and have a team that would rewrite basketball history. But neither of us took any chances. Team Joe's last three bench guys are Wah Wah Jones, Kenny Walker, and Aaron Harrison. Jones was a rugged mountain man from Harlan who was an All-SEC basketball player and an All-SEC wide receiver for Bear Bryant. He would scrap and rebound and generally make life torture for his opponents. Walker is only the second-highest scorer in UK history. He'd be instant offense, if Team Joe somehow bogged down. And Aaron Harrison is just the greatest big-shot scorer in UK history. If Team Joe has to have a 13th guy, then they will take a guy who could sit for 39 minutes, come in cold, and drain a three to beat the other team. That's Aaron.

Team Ryan went in a different direction. Because you can never have too many skilled seven-footers, he went for big DeMarcus Cousins off his bench. Admittedly, DeMarcus showed us what he could do in the post offensively and defensively, and in one year, showed himself to be nothing short of great. For his other two spots, Ryan took two pure shooters. One is Jodie Meeks, who just set the single-game scoring record while playing with Patrick Patterson and a bunch of guys who might've stumbled in from the YMCA. The other is Vernon Hatton, who is right there with Aaron Harrison on a list of all-time clutch Wildcats. All he did was drain big buckets.

Who is coaching? It probably wouldn't matter if the two of us did. The tendency is to say that Coach Rupp gets the job, and there can be no doubt he would've loved to have a run-and-gun-capable team like this. But who is really the only guy who is going to balance minutes among 13 great, great players? Yup. It's John Calipari. Our semi-official guess is that he brings in Rupp to install the offense, and then he can focus on defense.

So noted below are our respective UK dream teams. Take your best shot. We'd take it kind of easy on your team, because they are UK guys. But they are going down.

Team Joe		*Team Ryan*
Ralph Beard	PG	John Wall
Tony Delk	SG	Tony Delk
Jack Givens	SF	Jamal Mashburn
Jamal Mashburn	PF	Dan Issel
Anthony Davis	C	Anthony Davis

Second Team		
John Wall	PG	Ralph Beard
Louie Dampier	SG	Rex Chapman
Tayshaun Prince	SF	Jack Givens
Dan Issel	PF	Kenny Walker
Bill Spivey	C	Bill Spivey

Rest of Bench		
Wah Wah Jones		DeMarcus Cousins
Kenny Walker		Jodie Meeks
Aaron Harrison		Vernon Hatton

Celebrate!

WHERE: In most instances, downtown Lexington, Kentucky, intersection of Euclid and Woodland. Or maybe a Final Four site.

WHEN: August until March

HOW TO DO IT: Go to a big game. Go to a game that seems like an impossible win. Or just drive to Lexington.

COST FACTOR: Solidly $$ or $$$ per person, maybe closer to $$$$ if you want a prime seat at a game. Or $: just gas money to get to Lex Vegas.

DIFFICULTY FACTOR: Getting to a big game is difficult. But just joining the crowd? No problem at all.

BUCKET RANK:

HINTS FOR LITTLE WILDCATS/RELUCTANT WILDCATS: Probably not a great idea for little ones to be here, though we have seen children having a great time. In terms of safety, we suggest letting them watch the celebration on television

- -

Rest assured, I had a plan when UK looked to be in prime position to win its eighth national championship.

At the time I was working for a college in northern Kentucky, but I was also running a UK fan blog for the *Cincinnati Enquirer*. The blog, which I had run for three years, had allowed me to attend all the home games that season and I had a blast. But I wasn't able to follow the team on the road. I have a family, and I didn't want to be away from them for three weeks. The Final Four was in New Orleans, so I was watching on television like all the other fans. But I'd decided that at the end of the first half, if UK was playing well and it looked like the Cats were going to win, I was going to hop in the car and drive an hour down to Lexington to be a part of the celebration. Where else would you want to be?

At the end of the first half of the 2012 national championship game, Kentucky led Kansas 41–27.

By this time it was around 10:30 PM and my wife and daughter had already gone to bed, so I kissed them good night and got in the car. And all the way down to Lexington I was so nervous about the second half I couldn't even listen to it. I decided to turn on the radio as I approached the Lexington city limits. Then I heard Tom Leach saying it was over and that we'd won. Immediately, from seemingly all corners of the downtown skyline, I saw fireworks start to go off. Lexington was alive. I'll never forget it.

What better way can any player or coach celebrate than by getting a championship ring? Each year, the NCAA gives players championship rings (modest by most standards—gold rings with a simple black face, and gold NCAA lettering on the top). But teams normally buy rings for the players, too. Here you see replicas of the 1996 ring (left) and the 2012 ring given to the players. (Ryan Clark)

Like hundreds of thousands of other UK fans, I took to the streets that night, giddy with celebration energy. Some of the traditions after celebrating a national championship include the burning of old couches. That was done.

The one thing that really surprised me was driving through downtown. I had the windows rolled down. The night was comfortable. I purposely passed through downtown right in front of Rupp Arena, and people just poured out of the local restaurants and bars, filling the streets. It was like Mardi Gras—except, there were grandparents in the street too, dancing with their little grandchildren. It was just pure joy.

The night was not without some crazy scenarios. One person was shot in the leg. Others were arrested for being too wild. But on the whole, it was an experience all fans should see.

I ultimately met up with some friends there and we went to the place everyone goes—the corner of Woodland and Euclid Avenues—and yes, a couch was burned. But much more frequently, I just saw pure happiness. Celebrating a big game or a national championship is something everyone needs to be a part of.

As an aside, after Kentucky's national title, as well as its runner-up finish in 2014, the university held celebrations the following afternoon in Rupp Arena. Typically, posters are given out as well, and thousands of fans show up to recognize the achievement of the season. The events are free to all they can fit into the arena—and it's about an hour-long event that should not be missed.

In the past, fans have also waited outside the Lexington airport and greeted the team when it returns from their tournament run. People have also lined the streets to wave to the bus that takes the team from the airport to Rupp Arena. There is no limit, it seems, to what the Big Blue fans will do to show their love.

Like everything else in this book: If you get a chance, do it.

—Ryan

EXTRA POINTS

UK Plays Football, Too, and We Can Prove It

In the previous chapter we mostly described what it was like to celebrate a big basketball win. What about in football?

Because of the few huge football wins in program history, if you're lucky enough to see one, you tend to celebrate it a little more. Or a little crazier.

Joe and I have been lucky enough to see a few. The best year seemed to be 2007. Joe was able to watch UK beat No. 9 U of L when Cats quarterback Andre Woodson found Stevie Johnson on a long bomb for a game-winning touchdown. He loves to tell the story of everybody in his section jumping up and down so much that nobody was still in their actual seat area. You'd look around and the guy who was behind you was three rows in front of you, and the lady who was beside you was across the aisle somewhere.

Later that season, we both watched Kentucky defeat No. 1 LSU in triple overtime.

That was a different kettle of fish. Everyone seemed to not really know what to do. We were all just jumping up and down, amazed. We couldn't really believe it. Fans started jumping onto the field, and running around. Joe and I decided against that. We did make sure to get a picture with everyone celebrating in the background, to memorialize the occasion. I also took a pic of the scoreboard.

While most of the fans took to a goalpost and pulled it to the ground, it was nothing like the scene in 1997 when UK quarterback Tim Couch threw a game-winning touchdown to Craig Yeast to beat Alabama in overtime. At that time, goalposts were not bendable like they are now. Now—as it was during the Louisville and LSU wins—fans can bring down a goalpost, but it won't go anywhere. Back in 1997, fans could bring down a goalpost, detatch it, and carry it off.

That's what happened after the Alabama win. Legendary columnist Chuck Culpepper of the *Lexington Herald-Leader* decided to follow, to see where the broken goalpost would end up. Part of it was found—of course—in a frat house.

The Alabama victory was the first time the goalposts came down at Commonwealth Stadium. Incidentally, it was also the last time UK beat the Crimson Tide.

In summary, if you ever find yourself in a historically significant UK sports situation, go celebrate with your like-minded fans. Grab a piece of dirt to save. Hop on a goalpost. Watch as others burn a couch. More than anything, use your camera phone. Or use someone else's camera phone. Take a selfie—or another picture. Take dozens. You're going to be happy you did.

Chapter 6

The Big Blue Beyond

As our time together comes to an end, we wanted to close out your UK Wildcat Bucket List with a few items that are special. From considering our own UK heroes to thanking the man who integrated SEC football, from considering God and basketball to remembering what not to do as fans, these items are a little more serious, but very much important parts of UK fandom.

Draw Up Your UK Mount Rushmore

Ryan and I are sports fans, and we're guys, so one thing that never gets old is classifying—the best, worst, most memorable, least memorable, etc. But there's one argument that never fails. Ever since Gutzon Borglum shaved four U.S. presidents into the side of a South Dakota mountain, people have reconfigured their own Mount Rushmore. And why stop at U.S. presidents? What about a Mount Rushmore of great actors? Of American sitcoms? Of the best bands ever? The limits are truly endless.

But we're Cat fans, so the pivotal Mount Rushmore considerations are those involving UK. Here's a couple of UK Mount Rushmores—because if you're going to mentally chip away a ton of stone on the side of a fictional mountain, why do it just once?

Ultimate UK Mount Rushmore:

Adolph Rupp: Sure, he won 876 games. And four NCAA titles. And was a five-time coach of the year. But the real reason the Man in the Brown Suit is a must is that the entire culture of UK basketball starts with Adolph Rupp. Don't believe me? Can you imagine going to the Mauer Arena to watch games? That's where UK was, before Rupp. And we'll be waiting a long time to see another coach win four titles in Lexington.

Cawood Ledford: There were great broadcasters before (Claude Sullivan) and great broadcasters since (Tom Leach), but for longevity and ability to capture the heart of his listening audience, no one ever touched Cawood Ledford. He spent more than three decades calling UK games, with more than two decades as the first network exclusive "Voice of the Wildcats." Even if another great broadcaster comes along, it won't be the same in the age of widely available television.

Bill Keightley: He never made a jump shot, never called a timeout, but he was an equipment manager from 1962 to 2008. The players loved him, and the fans always felt that he embodied the entire Big Blue Nation. For all those who survived from Rupp to Gillispie, Keightley was a reminder of past greatness and a promise of its return.

A.B. "Happy" Chandler: He was a player, but at Transy, not UK. The two-time Kentucky governor made probably his greatest athletic mark as the commissioner of Major League Baseball who encouraged the integration of the game. But he's a Wildcat legend and was a noted confidant of Adolph Rupp. But he's on the mountain because he sang "My Old Kentucky Home" like no one has, before or since. Chandler died in 1991, but his passionate Senior Day renditions, some available on YouTube, can still produce a shiver or a tear.

UK Basketball Players Mount Rushmore:

Ralph Beard: His free throw won UK's first NIT in 1947. He won two more NCAA titles and an Olympic gold medal, and his ability to run and gun not only outclassed Bob Cousy, but foreshadowed the future of basketball. Many have tried, but none has done it better.

Dan Issel: The leading scorer and rebounder in the history of UK basketball, and in three seasons, the man they called "The Horse" wasn't always flashy, but he could play the game. Consider—in his senior year, 1970, he was held to fewer than ten rebounds only twice, and to under 20 points only once.

Jamal Mashburn: Like Beard, Mash was a culture changer. He was Rick Pitino's first big recruit, and his game, full of finesse and power, shooting ability, and rough-and-tumble post ability, was unstoppable. His success after basketball should also be a reminder to those who follow in his footsteps.

Anthony Davis: Words simply fail. Davis was the greatest defensive player of our lives, if not ever. His offensive skills were never forced, and could shock with their smoothness. When will we ever see another guy who can block shots like Bill Russell, and pop out on the wing and drain a perimeter jump shot?

UK Football Mount Rushmore:

Paul "Bear" Bryant: He led UK to its greatest season ever in 1950. He brought in most of the great players in UK lore, and he went 60–23–5 in eight seasons in Lexington. Losing him to Texas A&M is always the great "What if?" of UK football.

Vito "Babe" Parilli: His steady play at QB led UK to a three-year run of Orange, Sugar, and Cotton Bowl appearances—and a 2–1 record in the games. He led the SEC in passing for three years, and his 50 touchdowns was the school record for almost half a century.

Art Still: The greatest defensive player in UK history, Still was a huge, athletic defensive end who was probably fifteen years ahead of his time. He terrorized quarterbacks and throttled running backs, and led UK to two great seasons in the late '70s.

Tim Couch: The pride of Hyden, Kentucky, was proof that the biggest-scale recruit in the land could stay home and play for the Wildcats—and succeed. In two years under Hal Mumme, Couch racked up more than 8,000 yards and 70 touchdowns. He led UK to its last major bowl appearance in 1999's Outback Bowl. He was the first pick in the 1999 NFL Draft, and today is a successful TV analyst.

Non-Football/Men's Basketball UK Mount Rushmore:

Valerie Still: What can you say about the greatest UK women's basketball player ever? 2,763 points, 1,525 rebounds, and a career of absolute domination are Still's accomplishments.

A.J. Reed: In 2014, UK had perhaps the best hitter and the best pitcher in college baseball. Both were A.J. Reed. Reed, a huge first baseman, hit .336 with 23 home runs in just 223 at bats…and also went 12–2 with a 2.09 ERA as a pitcher. Mount Rushmore worthy, for sure.

Jomo Thompson: Sorry, coach Rupp, but just four NCAA titles? Coach Thompson has eight as the head coach of UK cheerleading.

Thompson also was part of three NCAA champion cheer squads during his own cheering career at UK.

Jenny Hansen: I've got to be honest. I thought she should go on the list when she was announced at a UK football game as a UK Athletics Hall of Fame member and promptly did a somersault. I'm told that Jenny was a thirteen-time All-American, and was a star gymnast at UK. I don't even understand how that is possible. Did she clone herself? Regardless, she's a legend beyond my understanding.

—Joe

. . . .

Visit Adolph Rupp's Grave

WHERE: The Lexington Cemetery, right down the road from Rupp Arena, 833 West Main Street.

WHEN: Visiting hours are 8:00 AM–5:00 PM daily

HOW TO DO IT: Easy to get to. You could go before a game. You could go when the weather is pretty or the moment strikes you.

COST FACTOR: Free

DIFFICULTY FACTOR: There are normally many visitors.

BUCKET RANK:

HINTS FOR LITTLE WILDCATS/RELUCTANT WILDCATS: Not a great event for kids. Cemeteries can, in general, be a little creepy, and this one is no different. It's big and beautiful, and children could run around, but we don't advise bringing little ones on this trip.

. . . .

As the sun set, and the clock ticked closer to 5:00 PM, I knew I only had a few moments.

I was determined. So many people had told me I needed to go see Coach Rupp's grave. One day I had some free time so I decided to go over. It was kind of a creepy day, which seemed like an appropriate time to visit a cemetery. It was a gray day in the fall, filled with leafless trees and dark clouds. It was chilly too, and there was a breeze that made you want to wrap your coat around you.

I pulled into Lexington and headed toward the cemetery, having never been there before. It's really not far from downtown or Rupp Arena, which is probably as it should be.

I pulled up to the gate and met a police officer. He was very kind. I told him I wanted to see Coach Rupp's grave, and he told me where it was located. He made sure to remind me that I didn't have a whole lot of time, and I acknowledged that I understood. I said I just wanted to pay my respects and take a few pictures. The guard told me to make sure and be back by 5:00 PM.

We suggest you visit Adolph Rupp's grave in the fall, as the sun is setting. It's spooky and quiet and makes for great pictures. And it's located just down the street from Rupp Arena. (Ryan Clark)

As if to underline his insistence, he told me that I did not want to be locked in the cemetery overnight. I agreed, and made sure to heed his warning.

The site is actually very tranquil and pretty.

"Many consider the grounds to be beautiful in their own right," the cemetery website says. "We are proud of this, and take seriously the responsibility of maintaining its artistic and natural beauty; that's why we insist on setting aside sixty percent of the cost of a burial site for perpetual care. It's one part of our commitment to keeping the Lexington Cemetery as beautiful and affordable in the future as it is today."

I enjoyed the drive out, and having the chance to view one of the big pilgrimage sites of UK basketball fandom. After I found the appropriate section of cemetery, I got out of my car and walked the remaining distance.

It was completely quiet. No birds. No other cars or people around. I chose a pretty spooky time to go. But it was very peaceful. It seemed like a very nice place for the legendary coach to be, not far from the arena that bears his name.

I was surprised by the simplicity of the headstone. To be honest, I expected some big mausoleum, but there are larger, more ornate markers in the immediate area. Coach Rupp's marker is very tasteful, decorated with a basketball in the center.

Underneath the coach's name, there are four lines that represent a perfect tribute to his legacy:

U.K. Basketball Coach 42 Years
Olympic Coach 1948
Four N.C.A.A. Championships
National Basketball Hall of Fame

Not a bad few things to have on your headstone.

WE'RE SURE HE WAS A UK FAN, TOO

As long as we're seeing grave sites of famous Kentuckians, go see Daniel Boone's grave site at the Frankfort Cemetery. We're pretty certain he would have loved UK's sports teams, too. "From the grave, you get a scenic view of the Kentucky River," the *Lexington Herald-Leader* says. After a tense argument with the town of Marthasville, Missouri (which also claims ownership of Boone's remains and has its own grave site), it seems Kentucky has won out. Official documents in 2010 reveal the Kentucky site to have at least some of Boone's remains. It's worth a look: Frankfort Cemetery, 215 E. Main Street, Frankfort, Kentucky. Hours: summer: 8:00 AM.–8:30 PM; winter: 8:00 AM–5:30 PM daily.

I took a picture or two, said a prayer and a few words of thanks, took in the scene again, and quickly made my way back out. I wanted to check another box off of my personal UK bucket list, but I did *not* want to get stuck in Lexington Cemetery overnight.

On December 10, 1977, Rupp died in Lexington of complications from cancer. He was 76. Coincidentally, Kentucky defeated Kansas that night in Lawrence, in a game billed as "Adolph Rupp Night." Less than four months later, Joe B. Hall (who took over for Rupp as head coach at UK) won the school's fifth national championship.

In 2009, John Calipari coached UK to its 2,000th victory. Leading up to that milestone, on a rainy Lexington day, he made a pilgrimage to Rupp's grave with Hall and Rupp's son, Herky. At that point, UK had won a total of 1,998 games. He filmed a portion of the visit for his television show, "This Is Kentucky Basketball."

"More than half the wins were from your father, and you as an assistant, coach, and player," Calipari told Herky and Hall. "More than half of them!"

The three placed poinsettias and a wreath near the base of the headstone before leaving.

—Ryan

. . . .

Meet Your Wildcat Hero

I met my Wildcat hero by complete accident. Our paths hadn't exactly been destined to cross. The game that forever cemented me as a diehard Wildcat fan happened to also be his last game. I barely caught his UK career, and only after it was over did I realize what I had missed.

Once he was finished at UK, he wasn't exactly in the public eye. On the day that I met him, it had been months, if not years since I had thought about him. But I walked through the door of the Cumberland National Guard Armory, where I had come to hear second-year UK football coach Hal Mumme discuss his current squad, and there he stood. I did a double take. It was him, all right.

I approached the table where he stood. It was covered with name tags, doubtlessly intended to make us all more comfortable at Coach Mumme's speaking event. I couldn't resist. "This guy," I said to the lady behind the table, indicating my Wildcat hero, "probably doesn't need a name tag."

And Cawood Ledford smiled at me.

He was born in 1926, in the hills of eastern Kentucky, one county over from where I grew up several decades later. He was the son of a coal miner, and I am the grandson of one. Fresh off his wartime service in the U.S. Marines, Ledford graduated from Centre College, and quickly followed in the footsteps of Claude Sullivan, making a career broadcasting Kentucky sports on the radio.

In this era, there was no single UK network. A multitude of announcers would simultaneously broadcast the games, and in spinning the dial, a listener might hear Cawood, Sullivan, J.B. Faulconer, and Dee Huddleston all describing the same game. But over time, Sullivan and Ledford became the two biggest voices in UK broadcasting. When throat cancer took Sullivan's life in 1967, Cawood Ledford became the leading light in UK sports. A couple of years later, he became *the* voice of UK athletics, as the single-broadcast network took hold.

He began as a contemporary of Rupp, and the fans who depended on him to be their eyes in the pretelevision days never forgot Ledford. To this day, my great-uncle, Charles Banks, is still known in his family as "Cawood" for his unfailing devotion to his favorite broadcaster. By the time I came to know his voice, Ledford had expanded far beyond UK sports. Ledford was a legendary horse-racing announcer, and called events as diverse as boxing matches, golf, and baseball's World Series.

But it was in the early years of Rick Pitino's Kentucky–Camelot era that I became acquainted with Cawood. His flawless syntax and delivery, his clear and emotive voice, and his ability to be at once incredibly professional and still comfortable in his own skin sold me. Players came and went. Cawood stayed.

Until he didn't. The heartbreaking loss to Duke in 1992 was his final UK game, as he retired with Adolph Rupp's last line serving as his own—"For those who traveled the glory road with me, my eternal thanks." *Sports Illustrated* noted that Ledford had worked the Final Four the following week, and someone had said something to him

Several Wildcats have proved over the years that they are more than just talented players. On weekends, mostly when the media is nowhere to be seen, players like Willie Cauley-Stein travel to area hospitals to spend time with sick children. Oftentimes those relationships extend beyond one simple trip. There are many fans—some who are very, very young—who claim Willie to be their Wildcat hero. (Tim Sofranko)

then about doing his last game. He corrected his well-wisher by saying, "I did my last game last week."

In the fall of 1998 when I met him, Cawood was still eminently recognizable. He was very much in his element that night, nattily attired, in excellent voice, and introducing Coach Mumme with well-chosen remarks. I don't even remember exactly what I said to him, or what he said to me. When I think of Cawood's voice, I think of him saying "Got it!" or "That one had a lot of iron on it, but it finally fell." But I remember that he was exactly like I thought he would be, polite and kind, and kind of regal. I know he smiled at me, that I thanked him for his excellent work, and that I'm glad I met him.

Cawood Ledford passed away in 2001. He had been acclaimed by U.S. presidents, and his death was noted in the *New York Times*. Rupp Arena's floor was subsequently designated Cawood's Court, and a banner with Cawood's microphone hangs in the rafters of Rupp Arena. Take time to notice that banner—maybe point it out to your children or grandchildren. Remind them that those hallowed rafters don't belong to just the All-American point guards or the seven-foot centers who dunked all over people, but that there's at least one spot that went to a man who spoke, in his own unique way, for all of Kentucky basketball.

That man was my Kentucky hero.

—Joe

• •

Portions of this story ran on KyForward.com and KentuckySportsRadio.com in 2014:

It was the winter of 1993 and I was 13 years old. I was in Lexington, ready to watch my beloved Kentucky Wildcats play a college basketball game.

I hadn't exactly paid to get into the game. See, I was lucky. As I explained previously in the "Ultimate Game Day Experience" section, because my aunt worked for the student newspaper at Kentucky, I was recruited to help pass out newspapers before the game. For my efforts I was able to get into the arena. I never had a seat, but hey, I was at the game.

When my distribution duties were finished I was able to roam freely, watch the pregame shootaround, and interact with all the Wildcat players I'd seen on TV. For that particular game I grabbed a large Wildcat sign so I could collect autographs.

With about 30 minutes still to go before game time, other Cats were out practicing their jumpers. But one player—a beefy, 6'9" guy with a buzz cut and big smile—was talking to some fans. I knew who he was—I knew all the players on my favorite team. I waited until he stopped chatting and asked if he'd autograph my sign.

"Sure, buddy," he said.

Other names on that sign would become more famous.

Jamal Mashburn. Tony Delk. Travis Ford.

But Todd Svoboda was the first to sign it. Later on I'd find out about his struggles, his achievements, and just how great a guy Todd could be.

Todd was a part of an engineering program at Northern Kentucky University where he stayed three years at NKU, then transferred to UK for the last two. It meant he had to say goodbye to a promising Division II basketball career, where he'd made a name for himself. He could be the conference player of the year if he played a senior season at NKU.

Instead, he transferred to UK, where he attempted to walk on to one of the best basketball programs in the country. For months Todd worked with the team, going through NBA-like workouts, all the while knowing it may be for nothing. It lasted until just before the start of the season. Then, Pitino and the team congratulated him: He'd made it.

A group of high school and college All-Americans swarmed him, slapping him high-fives and patting him on the back. He was on the team—and he couldn't have picked a better time. The Wildcats would go on to win 30 games, and Todd would have two unforgettable moments: one where he outscored future NBA star Allan Houston 4–3 in a win over Tennessee, and another where he hit a three-pointer at the very end of a blowout win over Florida State in the NCAA Tournament's Elite Eight round.

In his one season at UK, he was Final Four bound. So, you can see why, when I wrote a book about UK basketball, I would want to feature Todd in it. He had a great story.

After the book was released in 2007, I asked several of the players involved if they would like to come out to a book signing with me in Lexington. This is always a tough sell, because I'm not paying them anything. It's just a meet-and-greet for those players who want to interact with fans.

In short, two players said yes. Then, one of them backed out. The one who came? Todd Svoboda. He had become a chemical engineer working in Lexington and he brought his wife and children.

I brought my wife, and we found their family to be charming. We became closer, and talked often. I told him I was interested in nominating him for NKU's athletic Hall of Fame. He reminded me that he was a tennis champ there, too.

I saw him again at UK's alumni game in 2013. He yelled my name from across Rupp Arena and we shook hands. We chatted again and I couldn't believe how much his daughter had grown. He had three kids by then, ages 15, 13, and 4.

By then we felt more like friends.

Lastly, I remember when I heard Todd had cancer. After all, you remember things like that when they happen to people you care about.

It was early June. UK athletics director Mitch Barnhart tweeted the news, and I was shocked. I emailed Todd to see how he was and he told me to call. I feared the worst.

At 42, he sounded tired when I rang. He told me he'd noticed a node on his knee back in February. It was osteosarcoma, an aggressive bone cancer mostly found in teenagers or the elderly. It wasn't hereditary; Todd said doctors told him it was just bad luck.

For the past several months he's been in and out of chemotherapy at UK's Markey Cancer Center. Pitino called to check on him, as have other friends and fans.

He had to have his knee replaced, he told me. And the worst part of it all was the severe nausea. Well, maybe not the very worst.

"I won't play competitive tennis again," he said. "But I can probably go and hit some, taking it easy."

A year later, his treatment has worked. Todd once again fought a hard battle and he is winning. He says he's in "surveillance mode"— basically making sure the cancer doesn't come back.

"My faith has definitely helped me through this," he said. "Leg is doing better. Still need to strengthen it more but I am getting around okay. I just walk a little slower than before. The thing I'll miss the most is playing competitive tennis."

It looks as if Todd has headed this thing off at the pass.

He's better. He's gotten his energy back. And we still talk from time to time.

I consider him a friend.

But more importantly, I think of him as my UK hero.

—Ryan

Say "Thank You" to Nate Northington

There are players who are remembered because of their accomplishments. They pile up points like Jamal Mashburn, blocked shots like Anthony Davis, rebounds like Valerie Still, touchdowns like Randall Cobb. There are others who are remembered for their attributes—for intensity like Wesley Woodyard, for quiet confidence like Tayshaun Prince, for courage like Aaron Harrison. But there are other players who change the game simply by their very presence. Nate Northington was one of these.

Because had Nathaniel Northington not become the first African American athlete to sign athletic scholarship papers with an SEC school, had he not become the first African American football player in the SEC, had he not endured traumatic loss and hateful insults, then the names above might have meant nothing—at least, not in the context of ever being part of the University of Kentucky.

To meet him now is to meet an unimposing gentleman. Well dressed but not ostentatious, Northington could pass for a decade younger than he is. Reading glasses seem to be his only concession to the advance of years. He is polite and friendly, if somewhat reserved. In short, if you meet him and he is introduced as the regional director of property management with the Louisville Metro Housing Authority, you would probably take that at face value. It is only when one is reminded of exactly who Nate Northington is that the realization sets in that he is just too human for such a task. Perhaps it would be less unsettling if Northington were tall or hefty. He is neither. Or if he were angry or suspicious. He isn't. He is a man who looks like virtually any other, but who carried a burden that few could ever know.

He is a pioneer, a legend, and a UK treasure.

While the alleged racism of Adolph Rupp is still attached to UK by its detractors, an honest appraisal of the time and place shows that while UK was no better than its neighbors and competitors in integration, it was no worse either. Although *Brown v. Board of Education* should have been the death knell of racial segregation in public universities, the Jim Crow ("separate but equal") laws of the South were firmly entrenched. It was not until Lyndon B. Johnson signed the Civil Rights Act, and in so doing placed schools on notice that a failure to integrate could result in a loss of federal funding, that any sort of progress occurred on the front of integration of many schools in the deep South.

Nate Northington was the first African American to play football—and the first African American athlete in any sport—in the Southeastern Conference. We suggest you read his book, Still Running. *You won't be sorry.*
(Ryan Clark)

University of Kentucky President John Oswald, a Northerner by birth, was quick to answer the call to integration in the athletic arena. Now that Rupp is dead, evidence has slowly piled up to indicate that he was recruiting African American players, such as Wes Unseld and Butch Beard, even before the Civil Rights Act became the law of the land. The problem that Rupp faced is that while most people involved wanted African American athletes to become a reality, no one wanted to be the test case—the Jackie Robinson of the Southeastern Conference. In the meanwhile, Charlie Bradshaw and the football Wildcats attempted to break the color barrier, too.

Into this vacuum stepped Northington. An All-State football player at Thomas Jefferson High in Louisville, he planned to attend Louisville or Purdue—until Kentucky Governor Ned Breathitt summoned Northington to his mansion and delivered his pitch—he wanted Northington to be a Kentucky Wildcat, to be the first African American athlete in the SEC.

Northington signed, making history. Another African American player, Greg Page of Middlesboro, Kentucky, signed with UK a month later, and joined Northington on the team. Northington and Page roomed together as freshmen. By the rules of the time, freshmen were ineligible for varsity play, but the two played on the freshman team and were relatively well accepted by teammates. Page was the personality; Northington was friendly, but reserved. He came to do business, so to speak.

Business became more difficult early in his sophomore year. With both Northington and Page looking to play in actual SEC competition, disaster struck for Page. He was injured one day in a practice drill. What began as an injury ended up as paralysis, and 38 days later, as the death of Greg Page. A complex of residential apartments on UK's campus today bears Page's name. Northington felt isolated—haunted by Page's injury and the whispers that perhaps it was inflicted intentionally.

On September 30, 1967, Nate Northington played briefly in the defensive backfield in UK's 26–13 home loss to Ole Miss. The day before, he and his teammates had attended the funeral of Greg Page. Northington recalls talking to the walls of his empty dorm room, where Page's things sat as a sort of unintentional shrine.

Northington made it through five more games before the pressure became too much to bear. He struggled with a shoulder injury, and UK coach Charlie Bradshaw was notoriously tough on injured players. Northingon says the last straw came when coaches reprimanded him for missing classes by taking away his meal ticket.

Northington called the two freshman African Americans on UK's team, Wilbur Hackett and Houston Hogg, and asked them to meet him. He told them that they had to stay, and finish the work that he and Page had begun. And then Northington left, transferring to Western Kentucky University, where he played football and earned his degree.

Hackett and Hogg listened. Before his career at UK finished, Hackett was an All-SEC linebacker and a team captain. Slowly, but surely, Jim Crow was choked out of the playing fields. When Southern California, with an African-American quarterback and halfback, torched Bear Bryant's Alabama team 42–21 to begin the 1970 season, the end was in sight.

At Kentucky, Tom Payne became the first African American basketball player (placing UK second in the conference behind Vanderbilt in that integration effort). Within the decade, Jack Givens was an All-American and football stars Derrick Ramsey and Art Still led UK to its best season in a quarter century. All three are African American.

The 1980s brought Leonard Hamilton aboard as an African American assistant coach on the basketball squad, and in 1997, Orlando "Tubby" Smith became the first African American head coach of UK basketball. Less than a year later, he became the fifth UK coach to win an NCAA title.

TUBBY SMITH

Who: The successor to Rick Pitino for the UK head coaching position, the coach of UK's seventh NCAA Tournament champion

Why: If Nate Northington opened the door to people of color within UK's athletic program, by taking the most prestigious job in the Commonwealth of Kentucky, Smith blew it off the hinges.

Where to Find Him: These days, he's the head coach at Texas Tech. He's a busy man, but is noted for being incredibly personable.

Three decades after Northington made his debut, UK athletic director C.M. Newton found himself hunting for a head basketball coach. Rick Pitino had just led UK to back-to-back national title game appearances, but then bolted for the Boston Celtics of the NBA. It quickly became apparent to Newton that the man for the job was former UK assistant coach, and then–Georgia coach Orlando "Tubby" Smith.

Smith was hired and promptly set about the business of winning an NCAA title, which he immediately did in April 1998. The last glass ceiling at UK had been shattered. When it became obvious that Smith was the lead candidate for the job, an African American columnist at the *Lexington Herald-Leader* named Merlene Davis wrote a column asking Smith to turn the job down. She insinuated that in view of UK's racial issues in the past, Smith would be essentially terrorized if he lost.

Thankfully, Smith ignored the helpful wisdom. He coached for a decade at UK. While he never returned to another Final Four, he was a well-respected coach who was noted for developing players. His wife, Donna, was a visible force, cheering actively for the team at road games, and her reign as the First Lady of Kentucky basketball has never been matched. UK star Winston Bennett advised in 2013 that Smith's hiring, for him, was a moment not entirely unlike the election of President Obama. Times have changed. Black and white are irrelevant. Blue and white are what the BBN cares about.

Time has been relatively kind to Northington. He earned a degree—making him the fifth child in his family to do so. He is happily married and has done well professionally. Northington expresses no bitterness, saying he is only sorry that things didn't work out differently at UK.

But in recent years, at first slowly, but now with increased momentum, Northington's significance has been emphasized across America. At the University of Mississippi, where the National Guard had to be called in to integrate the school only four years before Northington signed with UK, coach Hugh Freeze invited Northington to come and address his team. Freeze thanked Northington for what he had done.

Former UK quarterback Paul Karem told columnist Dave Kindred recently, "Government programs didn't break down the barriers of race in the South. Neither did busing. Military intervention didn't do it and social engineering didn't do it. As much as anything or anybody, football did it. And who was first to do it? We were."

It was Nate Northington who handled the actual work. As time rolls on and the nation grows closer to becoming color-blind, it is hard to imagine that once upon a time, there was one young man who carried the hopes of integration on his shoulders and made them a reality.

In a sense, as a fan who grew up in an era when color mattered less and less, the sacrifices made by Nate Northington are beyond my comprehension. But when I met him in 2014, I shook his hand and I thanked him. I told him I appreciated what he had done, and that I understood that today wouldn't be possible without the work he had put in years before.

Any true-blue Kentucky fan should count it a privilege to do the same. If your path crosses with Northington, share your appreciation. And in the meanwhile, tell his story. Make sure that young African American athletes know about the guy who went first. Make sure that university decision makers know that Nate's courage is far from forgotten—and remind them that a statue of the man who broke the athletic color barrier in the SEC would look very nice around Commonwealth Stadium. And celebrate a Kentucky treasure. He was first, but thanks to his integrity and leadership, Nate Northington paved a path—and made sure that he was far from the last.

—Joe

. . . .

Remember the Cats Who Have Fallen on Hard Times

In Rupp Arena, Richie Farmer has a number. It's #32, and it hangs in the rafters, attesting to Farmer's skill and dedication in his four seasons as a Kentucky Wildcat. From 1988 to 1992, the Clay County native was one of the most beloved players on some of the most electrifying Kentucky teams of modern memory.

Today, Richie Farmer has another number. It's the inmate number that he wears at the USP Hazelton, a federal prison located in Bruceton Mills, West Virginia. It attests to his pleading guilty to two counts of misappropriating public funds during his tenure as state agriculture commissioner. If Farmer's basketball rise is the stuff of legend, his legal fall is the stuff of cautionary tales.

A few years after Farmer, Antoine Walker was a UK star. He played two seasons before leaving for the NBA, where he was a lottery pick by the Boston Celtics. Walker helped win a title at Kentucky, and was an All-Star in the NBA. He earned a total of more than $110 million during his professional career.

Now, in his later 30s, Walker has gone from rags to riches and back. He was arrested in the late 2000s on criminal charges related to gambling debts. Walker filed for bankruptcy, and now spends much of his time pleading for young athletes not to follow his fiscal path.

Rex Chapman, like Walker, was a two-year Wildcat before going pro and enjoying a lengthy NBA career. A native of Owensboro, Chapman had both small-town roots and all-American talent. He was one of the most popular UK players ever, and after his pro career, he worked for the Phoenix Suns and then as a television commentator.

But in September 2014, Chapman was arrested for allegedly stealing $14,000 worth of merchandise from an Apple Store in Scottsdale, Arizona. While he has not yet been tried for any charges arising from that incident, Chapman did enter a drug rehab program shortly thereafter, apparently for pain medication addiction. Chapman is busily working to rehabilitate his public image, but it remains a delicate proposition.

These stories are, unfortunately, much more common than people would like to realize. Tom Payne, the first African American basketball player at UK, has spent the majority of his life in prison for rape, and in his midsixties, is desperately seeking his release. In February 2015, he told the *Louisville Courier-Journal*, "When I die, I don't want this part of my life to be the only thing that's on my tombstone." The embarrassment of a painful fall from glory is a common theme to these stories. Former Cats Ed Davender and Derrick Miller have faced charges arising from a ticket-related theft scheme. Davender's jail uniform was later sold on eBay. Bedraggled former UK coach Billy Gillispie notably entered rehab after losing the UK job, amidst rumors of excessive behaviors at UK.

Unfortunately, while the majority of former Wildcats seem to find success and fulfillment, there are those who are less fortunate. Some are imprisoned, some are feeling financial pressures, some are struggling with addictions. And they all have to deal with the whispers, the pointed fingers, and the loss of dignity.

Recently, I logged on to an Internet group for UK fans. In a matter of minutes, I saw people—people who claimed to be Kentucky fans—saying that Farmer's jersey should be removed from the Rupp Arena rafters, and that Chapman did not exist to them. And while I cannot glorify the activities that have often caused or brought about difficult circumstances for former Wildcats, I also hope sincerely that those people who are dumping on the downtrodden are in the minority.

I hope that real Wildcat fans will remember the players who have fallen on hard times. Send them a note in prison, telling them that you remember one of their better days. Send up a prayer for those without money or security, or with addictions that challenge their lives. And take a few minutes to remember the good times. Remember when Tom Payne changed basketball forever at Kentucky, or when Rex dunked all over Louisville, or Richie made big free throws to hold off an SEC foe, or Antoine did his little shimmy after another big dunk. Because real fans remember the good times, but don't quit on their team in the bad times. Even—maybe especially—in the really bad times.

Of course, as UK basketball has surpassed the century mark, there is a tremendous number of former Wildcats who have passed away. This is as good of a time as any to remember all of the former Cats who are no longer with us. The following list—which is very much partial and incomplete—comprises just a few of the many Wildcats who are gone, but certainly not forgotten.

- Desmond Allison (1998–2000)
- Cliff Barker (1946–49)
- Ralph Beard (1945–49)
- Burgess Carey (1924–26)
- Mike Casey (1967–71)
- John Crigler (1955–58)
- John DeMoisey (1931–34)
- Phil Grawemeyer (1953–56)
- Alex Groza (1944–49)
- Basil Hayden (1919–22)

- Wah Wah Jones (1945–49)
- Tommy Kron (1963–66)
- Cawood Ledford (Broadcaster, 1953–92)
- Jim Line (1946–50)
- Shelby Linville (1949–52)
- Kenny Rollins (1942–48)
- Layton Rouse (1937–40)
- Adolph Rupp (Coach, 1930–72)
- Forest Sale (1930–33)
- Carey Spicer (1928–31)
- Bill Spivey (1949–51)
- John Stewart (1999 signee, who died before he ever reached UK)
- Marvin Stone (1999–2002)
- Claude Sullivan (Broadcaster, 1946–67)
- Mel Turpin (1980–84)

—Joe

· ·

Ponder the Mysteries of Faith and Basketball

When he was alive, Bill Keightley, longtime UK equipment manager and well-loved quasi-official Mr. Wildcat, could not stand the University of Louisville. When Rick Pitino called Keightley to ask his thoughts in 2001 on taking the U of L job, Keightley exploded, "Have you lost your damn mind?"

But in 2008, when Keightley suddenly passed away, it ended up that the officiating minister at his funeral was…the University of Louisville team chaplain.

It was true…and complicated, much like the union of faith and basketball. As faith is inherently subjective, it is difficult for anyone to claim peculiar expertise in the balance of Kentucky's beloved game and the worship of God. But here are a few stories from those who have balanced basketball and God, and their insights.

Father Ed Bradley is a native of Grayson County, Kentucky, and grew up with no idea that he would become a priest. An article in the *Evansville Courier & Press* indicated that a summer spent working in an impoverished area in Louisville changed Bradley's life and caused him to embark on a journey to become a Franciscan monk.

His life changed again when he became a close friend of coach Rick Pitino shortly after Pitino accepted the UK coaching job. Bradley became the UK team chaplain, a post that he held until Pitino left for the NBA in 1997.

Bradley ultimately agreed to become the chaplain of the Louisville Cardinals after Pitino accepted that post. Nonetheless, he officiated not only at Bill Keighley's funeral, but at Cawood Ledford's final ceremony in 2001.

In 2012, Father Bradley answered some questions that cut to the heart of the questions of faith and basketball. "I always just ask God to be with [the players] and help them play to the best of their ability," he told the *Portland Tribune*. "God loves [the opposing team] just as much….It's not going to be who God loves the most. It's the team that plays the best."

That said, while Father Bradley does not attempt to curry favor with God, he does use his position of high esteem within athletic circles to advance social causes of concern. Most notably, in 1994, he established the Daniel Pitino Shelter, a homeless shelter in Owensboro named in memory of Rick Pitino's deceased infant son.

More recently, Father Bradley was named chaplain at Owensboro Catholic High School.

For **Cameron Mills**, the path to spiritual impact came through basketball. The son of a UK letterman, Terry Mills, Cameron grew up yearning to become a Wildcat. He turned down a scholarship offer from Georgia and coach Tubby Smith to walk-on in Lexington. After two and a half years of sitting the bench, Mills became an impact player for the Cats, keying a run to a national runner-up finish in 1997 and providing depth and outside shooting in the 1998 run to an NCAA title.

But while Mills' teammates planned for the NBA, Mills had little doubt where his next step was. "I felt a call to ministry in my spirit when I was 12 years old," Mills admits on his official website. Mills sees his on-court success as an example of God utilizing his athletic success to further His ultimate message. "It was like a dream sequence," Mills explains. "Nobody saw it coming—least of all me."

Mills began traveling in and around Kentucky, speaking to groups about his experiences in faith and basketball. As of the early 2010s, Mills supplemented this work with a job with LHC Group, a healthcare group in Lexington. But he recalls that when he told people about his ministry, they assumed it would be a one-or-two-year diversion before his next step. Sharing his faith hasn't become a next step, so much as the commitment of his life for Mills.

He's glad to build on his name as a Wildcat for ministry purposes. "It's no secret the important role that athletics play in life and how exalted they are in the world," Mills admits. "My job is to get out of the way, preach the Word, and let the Holy Spirit draw people unto Him."

Mills continues to preach, and can be best followed via his website at http://www.cmm21.com.

For some, basketball has provided a platform into spiritual matters. For others, basketball has been a means of surviving spiritual difficulty. In 1958, Adolph Rupp's "Fiddlin' Five" won an NCAA title with an undersized bulldog of a center named **Ed Beck**. Beck was a devout Christian, who continued his basketball career in part to move on from the painful death of his wife, Billie. Late in Beck's junior season, his wife passed away from cancer.

Beck had been a second-team All-SEC player in 1957, but was understandably devastated at the loss of his wife. He later recalled her entreating him, "Ask God to use this disease for his honor and glory." Billie Beck's prayer was answered. After Ed won an NCAA title at UK, he went to seminary school and became a pastor.

Beck preached throughout the nation, finishing his career as pastor of a United Methodist Church, and is now retired in Arizona. He wrote a book about his late wife, and carried her memory through his pastoral career. Beck fondly recalled to Doug Brunk in *Wildcat Memories* the support of coaches Rupp and Lancaster and Governor Chandler, and how it helped him through his darkest hours. He also thanked the fans, calling the support "overwhelming" and saying the fans' reputation for bleeding blue was very true.

If all of the stories of faith and Kentucky basketball were chronicled, the reader would grow overwhelmed. Wildcats of virtually every religious creed have found support and encouragement in Lexington—whether Mormon (Mark Pope), Muslim (Nazr Mohammed), or Jewish (famous team manager Humzey Yessin). The common thread seems to be that while no one would seriously claim that God favors the Kentucky Wildcats, athletes and team support members appreciate the unique position that being part of the UK program affords, and utilize that position to a more accomplished, efficient version of themselves. Words like "blessing" and "unbelievable" surface frequently in the comments of the religious Wildcats in regard to their UK experiences. To credit those experiences to God seems scarcely to be a leap of faith.

A Few Things Not to Do

These tips are in no certain order. We just thought that in a book where we guide fans through some of the most important things they have to do, we might want to at least give one series of suggestions to the things they should *not* do. Anytime.

Without further ado, **do not:**

Get a championship-inspired tattoo before the final. We all saw the pictures of the guy who got a 2014 National Championship tattoo—before the season even started. UK went on to lose 10 games, and a streak of amazing finishes got them to the national title game, where they lost to UConn. While the guy was almost proved correct, we suggest you not do this. It's just too hard to win these things. We guess, if you want, you could do this afterward. Then again, the guy who got the tattoo for 2014 apparently kept it. So, there you go. Have a mistaken sports tattoo? Own it!

Grow a line beard of any kind. Really. It's what kids in high school do. Or the saddest subgroup of Louisville fans. They do it too. Maybe just don't do it for that reason. Everyone has full, bushy beards now (Joe's note: except Joe). Try one of those.

Wear a jersey if you're over 35. Jerseys should be reserved for framed autographs and little kids.

Stalk a player for an autograph. Anywhere. Not when they're eating. Not when they're walking to class. Not when they're at the mall. Let them have their time. Say hello and walk away. (This especially goes for grown men and women. If you're a kid, you can pretty much get away with anything you want, so go for it. But not if you're, say, 16 or older).

Get into a fight about the UK–U of L game at a dialysis clinic.
Remember: in the week leading up to when the two teams met in the
Final Four in 2012, two old men (one a Louisville fan, the other for
Kentucky) were waiting for their dialysis when they started swinging
at one another. Who won? Who cares—people loved to write about
this incident. But it was really just embarrassing for everyone.

Wear a flat-billed hat if you're over 25. They have an age limit.
You just look ridiculous. We really have nothing more to say about
this one.

Play backseat coach. Avoid second-guessing what your coach is
doing (especially if he or she has won a national title and has had a
reasonable amount of success). They know what they're doing. Trust
them. The players make plays. The coaches coach. Let them do it and
be thankful they're doing it for you.

Blame the officials. Yes, they may have been bad. But chances
are, they were bad both ways. They did not make your team lose.
Saying so just makes you sound weak. Tip your non-flat-billed cap
to the other team and lose graciously. Shake hands after the game.
Congratulate those who won. There's something to be said for
sportsmanship.

Blame the media. Yes, the media have opinions. Some don't like
your team or your coach. None of this should bother you. If you do
not like a journalist (or something he or she wrote or said) do not
read them anymore. Do not follow them on social media. A journalist
without a following is a nobody.

**Become more interested in your rival team (and their success)
than your own.** Again—that's what the worst Louisville fans do.
Don't get us wrong—you can always root against the Cards or the
Hoosiers or the Blue Devils. But don't get so caught up in what
they're doing that you forget to be happy about your own team.

Be uncivil to rival fans. This goes for whether you're at home or
away. We have seen what can happen when celebrations get out of

hand on the road (like against Indiana in 2012). We should feel the same way about these fans when they come into our house. (This also includes an afterword: Don't get drunk and be "that fan,"—the one who is so obnoxious you set the bad example for all the rest of us).

Click without thinking. Never send some nasty tweet or post to someone on Twitter or Facebook—not even a rival fan who tries to engage you. You don't make anyone look good. Just leave it alone. You're better than that.

Get violent after wins or losses. Remember: it's just a game. We love it, yes, but it's nothing more than that. There's no need to throw the remote, or let your blood pressure get out of control.

Let one upset keep you from enjoying your team and a season. You need to keep it all in perspective. Yes, losses hurt. In 2015, Kentucky's dream undefeated season ended at the hands of Wisconsin in the Final Four. But remember—in 2013 UK was losing to Robert Morris in the NIT. The Cats followed it up with two straight Final Four appearances. Not bad, right? Those seasons were amazing—and you should remember them that way.

Hope this helps! Go Big Blue!